mixing up memories

mixing up memories

a cookbook of family recipes

6-2008

by christy eichers

Beaver's Pond Press, Inc.

Cover Photo Courtesy of Party Crashers Photography, Inc.

ISBN 10: 1-59298-231-X
ISBN 13: 978-1-59298-231-8

Library of Congress Catalog Number: 2008925897

Printed in the United States of America

First Printing: 2008

12 11 10 09 08   5 4 3 2 1

Beaver's Pond Press, Inc.

7104 Ohms Lane, Suite 101
Edina, MN 55439
(952) 829-8818
www.BeaversPondPress.com

to order, visit www.BookHouseFulfillment.com
or call 1-800-901-3480. Reseller discounts available.

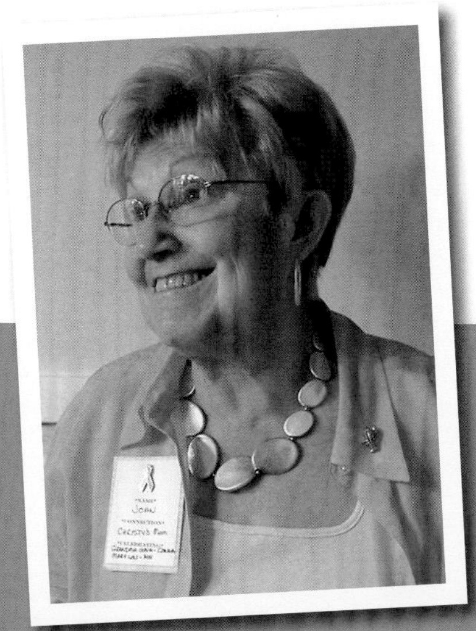

I'm dedicating this book to my Mom...
the woman who taught me how to cook.

We started cooking together when I joined 4-H in second grade and we are still swapping recipes.

Thanks for sharing this gift…
this love of cooking!

contents

introduction

A COLLECTION OF THE EICHERS FAMILY RECIPES

In the summer of 2007, two of my coworkers, Amy Draxten and Emily Haugen, came to me and said, "We know what we want for Christmas." Amy and Emily knew that I love to cook and entertain, so they asked me to compile all of my favorite recipes into a binder for them. Well, since they are both fabulous coworkers and I didn't want to disappoint them, I got to work and created a cookbook. I called that little collection of recipes, tips and stories *Christy's Kitchen Confidential*. Though I created a few extra copies for my family and friends, I was overwhelmed by the response I received from that little book. Everyone started to ask if they could buy additional copies. When I started the project, I never planned to sell *any* copies. I simply wanted to make a gift for my family and friends.

Then in early January 2008, I was driving home from Mayo. I had spent a couple days with my mom after she underwent a single mastectomy. Her surgery had gone very well, and I was in a good mood so I was blaring one of my favorite inspirational tunes off the *Wicked* soundtrack, "Defy Gravity." I played it over and over and was singing it at the top of my lungs… in my world, if you sing it louder, you sound better.

Throughout my trip, I kept thinking, what can we do to fight breast cancer? At some point, maybe when I was shouting the line of the song that says, "Some things I cannot change, but till I try I'll never know," the light bulb went off in my head. The previous Christmas, people had actually wanted to buy that little collection of recipes I had put together…what if my family put together a larger cookbook and all the proceeds went to the Susan G. Komen for the Cure®, a foundation that supports the fight against breast cancer? I went home and started researching. Just how much money could we actually raise? *Until we try, we'll never know.*

That is what this is…our attempt to raise funds to prevent breast cancer in future generations and to aid those who are currently battling breast cancer. All the funds generated from the sale of this book will go to the Susan G. Komen for the Cure® Foundation–Minnesota Affiliate.

Our family loves to cook and entertain. We share many laughs around meals and have created many memories in the kitchen. Throughout the book, I'll give you little glimpses into some of our favorite stories. We hope when you try these recipes with your family and friends, you'll be mixing up your *own* memories.

abbreviations

Unless otherwise noted, the following abbreviations appear in the recipes. All oven temperatures are given in Fahrenheit.

c. for cup(s)
in. for inch(es)
lb. for pound; lbs. for pounds
lg. for large
med. for medium
oz. for ounce(s)
pkg. for package; pkgs. for packages
pt. for pint(s)
qt. for quart(s)
sm. for small
T. for tablespoon(s)
t. for teaspoon(s)

appetizers

It's not really a party without some appetizers. In fact, some of our favorite parties are just buffets of appetizers. The problem with these types of parties? It is very difficult to "Step away from the BUFFET!"

Bacon and Swiss Appetizers

INGREDIENTS:

1 pkg. Pillsbury® Crescents
1-½ c. (6 oz.) shredded Swiss cheese
3 eggs, slightly beaten
¾ c. milk
1 T. chopped onion
8 slices bacon, cooked and crumbled
1 T. parsley flakes

DIRECTIONS:

Separate rolls and pat into bottom of 9x13-in. pan. Overlap edges and have them come up slightly on sides of pan.

Sprinkle cheese over top of dough.

Combine eggs, milk and onions. Pour mixture over cheese.

Sprinkle with bacon and parsley.

Bake at 425 degrees for 15 minutes. Cut into 2-in. squares; serve warm.

Chili Beef-Bean Dip

I remember when the Vikings used to be perennial winners...One year, Mom and Dad hosted a Super Bowl party in our orange basement. (You know, the basement with the paneling, orange shag carpet on the floor and even on some walls, and orange Formica on the paneled, wrap-around bar.) I remember getting the fold-out, double-wide RAMS & VIKINGS color-in insert from the *Tribune*. (I think it was just the *Tribune* at the time.) I colored it and hung it up on one of those paneled walls. One of our guests, Cathie Stordahl, brought the following taco dip. It was the very first taco dip I ever tasted and even after years of sampling taco dips, this is still one of my favorites.

INGREDIENTS:

1 lb. ground beef
½ c. onion
½ c. extra hot catsup
3 t. chili powder
1 t. salt
2 8-oz. cans kidney beans, with liquid
1 c. shredded sharp cheese
½ c. chopped stuffed olives
½ c. chopped onion

DIRECTIONS:

Brown beef and ½ c. onion together.

Add catsup, chili powder, and salt.

In a separate bowl, mash kidney beans and add beef mixture.

Transfer beef and bean mixture to a serving dish and top with cheese, olives and ½ c. chopped onion.

Cheese Ball

I'm sure these next two appetizers were also served at that Vikings Super Bowl party. Since my family is from Minnesota, we had to include at least one recipe with SPAM!

INGREDIENTS:

8 oz. cream cheese
1 sm. can Spam Spread
a dash salt
a little Worcestershire sauce
½ c. chopped pecans

DIRECTIONS:

Mash together all ingredients except pecans. Spread pecans on a large piece of plastic wrap.

Mound cheese mixture in middle of plastic wrap, on top of pecans.

Close up plastic wrap around cheese to form a ball.

Chill before serving.

Veggie Dip

INGREDIENTS:

½ c. sour cream
½ c. Miracle Whip®®
2 t. parsley flakes
1 t. dill weed
dash of salt and pepper
2 t. onion, minced
1-½ t. seasoned salt OR 2 t. Beau Monde Seasoning®

DIRECTIONS:

Mix together.
Chill until serving time.

Artichoke Dip

It would not be a party without my sister Annie's famous artichoke dip. This is the only appetizer her husband, Paul, ever requests. When it comes out of the oven piping hot, I can hardly wait to get into it and often burn my mouth with the first bite. Mom really likes it when Annie uses the food processor…she prefers the super-smooth dipping experience.

INGREDIENTS:

1 c. shredded mozzarella
1 c. shredded Parmesan cheese
1 c. mayonnaise
1 can artichokes, drained and chopped
1 can chopped green chiles

DIRECTIONS:

Preheat oven to 350 degrees.
Combine all ingredients in a food processor and blend until smooth. If you don't have a food processor, finely chop artichokes and mix all ingredients together.
Put in greased pie plate.
Bake for about 30 minutes. The dip should be golden on the top and bubbling.
Serve with wheat crackers, bread cubes, etc.

Cowboy Salsa

Annie claims this recipe as her own, but if pushed she'll admit she got it from Lynn Schleicher at an annual family gathering called the "Firecracker."

While most Minnesotans drive north to get to their cabins, Mom and Dad just head about twelve miles east of Mankato to Madison Lake. Dad has been going to this place since his neighbors Pink and Leone Meyer owned it when he was a little boy. At the first Fourth of July Firecracker, they decided we should have a naming contest: we needed to name the lake home. Our cousin's husband, Eric Evander, won the contest with his entry, "The Radisson on Madison." We've since nicknamed it, "The Rad on Mad." You'll see reference to this throughout this book, as Mom and Dad do loads of entertaining at the "Rad on Mad" each summer.

INGREDIENTS:

1 green pepper
1 red pepper
1 yellow pepper
1 orange pepper
4–6 stalks celery
1 red onion
1 can pinto beans
1 can black-eyed peas
1 can shoe peg corn

Marinade
1 c. oil
½ c. cider vinegar
½ c. sugar

DIRECTIONS:

Finely chop peppers, celery and onion. Drain beans and toss liquids.

Put chopped peppers and beans in a bowl.

Boil marinade ingredients and let cool.

Pour cooled marinade over peppers and beans and let sit for several hours.

Drain before serving. This can be refrigerated for a few weeks in the marinade.

Serve with corn chips or tortilla chips.

Dad and Grandma Gina frying fish at the Annual Firecracker Celebration

Salsa

We love my sister-in-law Melissa's salsa. It cracks me up when she brings it to the lake because she makes enough to fill one of those huge Pace® plastic containers, the ones with the handles. Let me tell you, Pace® has nothing on Melissa's salsa!

INGREDIENTS:

1 28-oz. can tomatoes chopped (drain some)

1 14-oz. can tomato sauce

1 can chopped jalapenos, drained

3 bunches of scallions

1 handful of fresh cilantro

2 cloves garlic

salt

pepper

DIRECTIONS:

Chop garlic, cilantro and scallions in a food processor.

If you like smooth salsa, add the tomatoes, sauce and jalapenos to food processor and chop. For chunkier salsa, combine the tomatoes, sauce, jalapenos and garlic/cilantro/scallions mixture in a bowl.

Salt and pepper to taste.

Guacamole

I love guacamole and needed to find the perfect recipe for this book. I made two of my favorites and took them to the Helgeson's beer tasting party. Everybody voted, and this recipe won.

INGREDIENTS:

4 ripe sm. avocados

1 lemon, juiced

8 dashes hot pepper sauce

½ c. sm. diced red onion

1 lg. clove garlic, minced

1 t. kosher salt

1 t. freshly ground black pepper

1 sm. to med. tomato, seeded and finely chopped

DIRECTIONS:

Cut avocados in half around the pit. Separate the halves. Pop out pit with spoon, then scoop flesh of avocados into a bowl.

Squeeze the juice of the lemon over the avocados.

Add pepper sauce, onion and garlic.

Mash using a fork and mix the ingredients into a chunky dip.

Add the tomatoes.

Mix well season with salt and pepper.

Serve with blue corn tortilla chips.

Brie en Croûte with Caramel and Walnuts (Brie in Puff Pastry)

Annie debuted this recipe at our 2008 "Cookies & Cocktails" cookie exchange party. While we were raving about it, she kept telling us it was very easy to make. As she says, "When you make this, it really makes you look like you know what you're doing in the kitchen." We hope you'll be able to impress your guests with this recipe.

INGREDIENTS:

1 8-oz. wheel of Brie
¼ c. brown sugar
¼ c. chopped walnuts
1 sheet puff pastry
1 egg beaten with 1 T. water

DIRECTIONS:

Trim rind off Brie and split in half crosswise. Spread the cut center of wheel with brown sugar and walnuts and put wheel back together like a sandwich.

Roll thawed puff pastry sheet to smooth out the wrinkles.

Wrap pastry sheet around Brie wheel like a package.

Trim bottom. Fold and pinch edges to seal the cheese in the puff pastry sheet. Place seam side down on a parchment-lined baking dish.

Brush with egg wash.

Bake at 400 degrees for 20 minutes. Pastry should be puffed and golden brown.

Serve with crackers or apple slices.

Note: You can decorate the top of the wheel with the scraps of puff pastry. Cut out shapes with cookie cutters and place on top of wheel before baking.

Rueben Dip

I made this for the first "Cousins' Christmas" gathering in 1999. Each year, Curt and Bud's offspring gather together the Sunday before Christmas to watch the Vikings and graze over a feast of appetizers. Uncle Curt really likes this one! (Probably because there are NO onions!)

INGREDIENTS:

8 oz. sour cream
4 oz. cream cheese, softened
15 oz. sauerkraut, drained
1 c. Thousand Island dressing
8 oz. Swiss cheese, shredded
20 oz. Budding® corned beef
rye bread party slices

DIRECTIONS:

Combine all ingredients.

Add to mini-slow cooker or mini-fondue pot.

Serve with crackers or rye bread party slices.

notes

Onion Brie Pinwheels

This is another recipe Annie unveiled during the 2007 holiday season. She brought them to "Cousins Christmas" and they received RAVE reviews from everybody except Uncle Curt and Paul. They wouldn't touch them!

INGREDIENTS:

2 med. onions, thinly sliced
3 T. butter
2 T. brown sugar
½ t. white wine vinegar
1 sheet frozen puff pastry, thawed
4 oz. Brie, softened and rind removed
1–2 t. caraway seeds
1 egg
2 t. water

DIRECTIONS:

In a lg. skillet, cook the onions, butter, brown sugar and vinegar over med.-low heat until onions are golden brown, stirring frequently. Remove onions with a slotted spoon. Cool to room temperature.

On a lightly floured surface, roll puff pastry into an 11x8-in. rectangle. Spread Brie over pastry. Cover with the onions; sprinkle with caraway seeds. Roll up one long side to the middle of the dough; roll up the other side so the two rolls meet in the center. Using a serrated knife, cut into ½-in. slices. Place on a parchment-lined baking sheet. Flatten to ¼" thickness. Refrigerate for 15 minutes.

In a sm. bowl, beat egg and water; brush over slices. Bake at 375 degrees for 12–14 minutes or until puffed and golden brown.

Makes 1-½ dozen puffs.

Veggie Pizza

This is a staple at all of our "Rad on Mad" gatherings. The thing I like best about my sister-in-law Melissa's veggie pizza is that she chops the veggies up very fine; she uses one of those choppers from Pampered Chef®.

INGREDIENTS:

2 pkg. Pillsbury® Crescents

2 8-oz. pkgs. cream cheese

1 envelope Good Seasons® Italian dressing mix

¾ c. Hellmann's® mayonnaise (not Kraft Miracle Whip®)

Finely chopped vegetables of your choice: broccoli, cauliflower, carrots, onion (optional and in small quantities)

2 c. finely shredded cheddar cheese

DIRECTIONS:

Spread crescent rolls out on a cookie sheet (like a pizza crust) and bake according to directions.

Mix cream cheese, dressing mix and mayonnaise until smooth.

Spread mixture on cooled crust and top with chopped vegetables of your choice; sprinkle with cheese.

notes

Stuffed Jalapenos

When Annie and Paul first moved to the suburbs, they hosted an annual party during the Chanhassen Winter Festival Ice Fishing Contest. Annie is a great hostess and she does so much to theme her events. Mardi Gras was the focus of this event, and she served Cajun food while we proudly hung our official ice fishing contest entries from beads around our necks. I remember having to take my niece Kayla to the outdoor biffy…oh, the layers of clothing we had to remove to get the job done! (Believe me, they've never worn so many clothes down in New Orleans!) While we enjoyed the festivities pre- and post-contest, some of the party-goers were serious about the event. One year, our pal George Rothsberg even won a prize. This recipe actually comes from his lovely bride, Mary Mettler.

INGREDIENTS:

12 jalapeno peppers
½ c. cream cheese
½ c. shredded mozzarella
½ c. grated Parmesan

DIRECTIONS:

Cut jalapenos in half the long way. Scoop out seeds.

Mix next 3 ingredients together.

Stuff cleaned-out jalapenos with cheese mixture.

Place on baking sheet and bake for 25–30 minutes at 350 degrees.

Chanhassen Winter Festival Ice Fishing Contest

Tuscan Hummus

In June 2007, I hosted a "Cooking for the Cure" party for Mom and my friend Donna Nicholson Svendsen. Both of them had undergone lumpectomies followed by radiation earlier that year. I guess that was my first venture raising money for Susan G. Komen for the Cure®. Thanks to my very generous family and friends, we raised over $2,300 to fight breast cancer.

INGREDIENTS:

8 cloves garlic
3 c. canned cannellini beans, drained
½ c. sesame paste (tahini)
6 T. olive oil
¼ c. freshly squeezed lemon juice
1 T. plus ½ t. soy sauce
1-½ t. salt
1-½ t. cumin
⅛ t. coriander
½ t. cayenne pepper
¼ to ½ c. cold water
pita bread

DIRECTIONS:

Chop garlic cloves in a food processor.

Add the beans and pulse a few times to chop them coarsely.

With machine running, pour in paste, followed by olive oil, lemon juice and soy sauce. Stop occasionally to scrape down sides of the bowl.

Add salt, cumin, coriander and cayenne.

Process until thoroughly blended. If it is too thick, add cold water.

Cover and refrigerate before serving with pita bread.

The guests of honor at my "Cooking for a Cure" party, Mom and Donna Nicholson Svendsen

Joel's Bull Bites

There is a great restaurant in Chanhassen called Axel's. They serve the best "bull bites." My brother, Joel, came up with this recipe and I think it's even tastier than the original.

INGREDIENTS:

3 lbs. cubed sirloin steak or stew meat

McCormick Gourmet Collection® Cajun Seasoning (whole bottle)

1 stick butter

DIRECTIONS:

Place Cajun seasoning in small bowl

Douse each cube of steak with Cajun seasoning and melt butter in a cast iron pan. Fry until cooked. Serve with a horseradish sauce (recipe follows).

MELISSA'S HORSERADISH SAUCE INGREDIENTS:

1 c. sour cream

¼ c. mayonnaise

2–3 T. horseradish

DIRECTIONS:

Mix all ingredients together.

notes

Mexican Fiesta Dip

This is a favorite from Mom. Once I start eating this, I can hardly stop myself! We've been known to dig out the leftovers for a midnight snack. When Mom and Dad hosted a Mankato High Class of '55 reunion party at the "Rad on Mad," one of Mom's classmates, Pat Murphy Anderson, brought this dip. Thanks, Pat!

INGREDIENTS:

1 15-oz. can black beans, drained
1 10-oz. can Rotel® diced tomatoes with green chiles, drained
1 11-oz. can Mexican-style corn, drained
1 8-oz. pkg. cream cheese, softened
shredded Monterey Jack cheese

DIRECTIONS:

Preheat oven to 350 degrees.
Mix together the first four ingredients and spread in a greased pie dish.
Sprinkle with shredded cheese.
Bake for 20 minutes.
Serve with tortilla chips.

notes

Fingerling Potatoes with Aioli

Mom and I have a tradition of spending an entire day at the Great Minnesota Get-Together, the Minnesota State Fair. Mom's been going to the fair since she was a little girl. My love of the fair comes from my many years in 4-H. One of the favorite things we like to do is watch all the demonstrations.

Sometimes we'll stand for hours watching the barkers peddle their gadgets. One year, we came home with "The Chopper." It was not our wisest investment. In fact, it became a little bit of a family joke. Some lucky family member found this wrapped up under the Christmas tree for a number of years. But one of our greatest purchases was Ginsu knives. What a deal; buy one and get one free. They even threw in that utility knife that the demonstrator used to cut an aluminum can in half! And I'm still using mine!

In 2006, I became mesmerized by the woman demonstrating the Bamix® hand mixer on the second floor of the Grandstand. After an hour-long demonstration and three easy payments, I am the proud owner of a Bamix® hand mixer. Simply put, it is the most amazing kitchen gadget…it takes the place of a mixer, food processor, blender and so many more appliances :). You'll need a Bamix® hand mixer to make the aioli. If you don't have one, just buy the aioli. Or you can download a blender recipe off of the Internet.

INGREDIENTS:

2-½ lbs. fingerling potatoes, unpeeled
kosher salt
1 egg, room temperature
1 t. dry mustard
½ t. salt
1 t. lemon juice
1 t. white vinegar
1-¼ c. canola oil
1–2 cloves garlic, minced
chives
additional salt and pepper, to taste
ALL ingredients MUST be at room temperature!

DIRECTIONS:

Rinse potatoes and put them in a lg. saucepan. Cover them with cold water, add 1 T. salt and bring to a boil.

Simmer uncovered for 15–20 minutes until they are just tender.

Drain the potatoes in a colander and cover with a kitchen towel, allowing them to steam for 5–10 minutes.

Place aioli ingredients in a container.

Place Bamix® wand with "B" blade to bottom of container, turn on and hold still for 12 seconds. Then simply raise the wand and push the oil down into the beaten egg.

Fold in minced garlic.

Slice potatoes in half and place them on a serving plate.

Sprinkle with salt and pepper and chives. Serve with aioli.

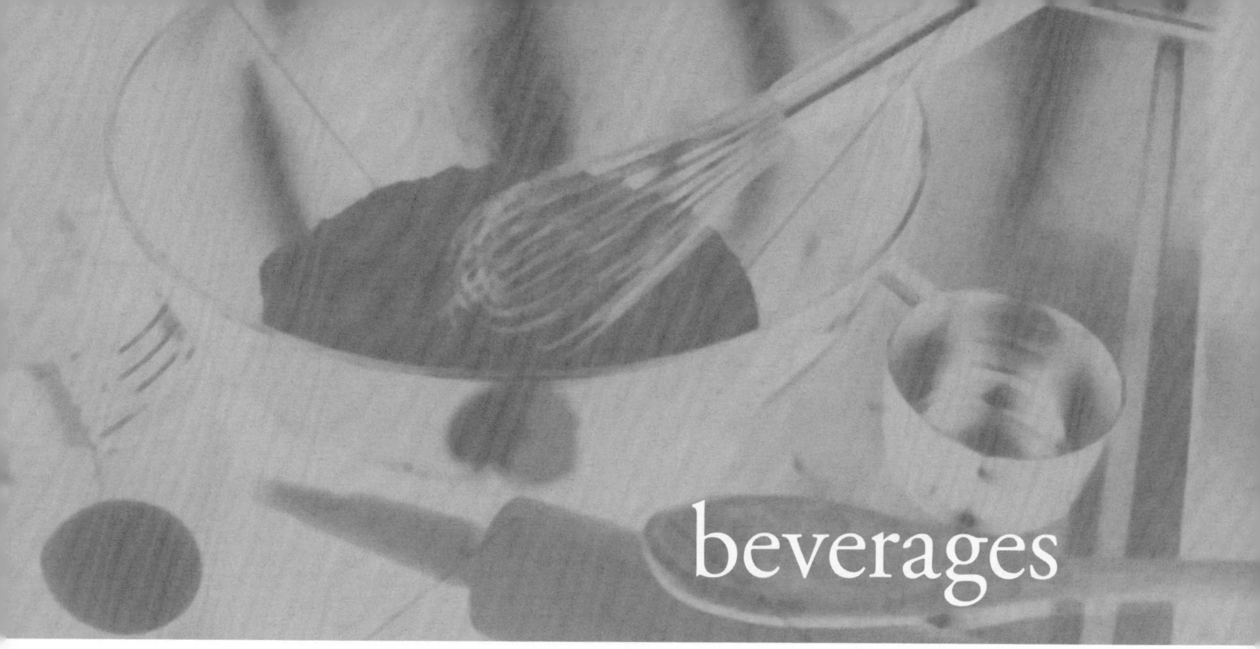

beverages

Pomegranate Cosmos

I hosted Christmas Eve in 2005 and served these festive cocktails. Just as Santa showed up, Melissa broke out in hives. She was allergic to the pomegranates. Thankfully, my neighbors had some antihistamine! We love these drinks; we just never serve them to Melissa anymore!

INGREDIENTS:

2 c. (16 oz.) good vodka

1 c. (8 oz.) orange liqueur (recommended: Cointreau)

1 c. (8 oz.) pomegranate juice (recommended: Pom Wonderful®)

½ c. freshly squeezed lime juice (about 3 limes)

lime peel strips, for garnish

DIRECTIONS:

Combine the vodka, orange liqueur, pomegranate juice and lime juice in a pitcher and refrigerate until ready to use.

Pour the mixture into frozen martini glasses; add a twist of lime peel and serve immediately.

Cosmos

After experimenting, I think Annie and I agree this is the way to make a Cosmo. I even ask for Absolut® Mandarin vodka when I order them out. That is definitely the secret ingredient.

INGREDIENTS:

Fill shaker with ice.

Add ¾ shot of each:

- Cointreau
- Rose's® lime juice
- Cranberry Juice
- Add 2–3 shots of Absolut® Mandarin vodka

DIRECTIONS:

Cover, shake, serve and ENJOY!

Cran-Ginger Cocktail

We served these for Thanksgiving 2007. They were very light and tasty.

INGREDIENTS:

1 c. frozen cranberries

1 lime, juiced

2 c. vodka

2 c. cranberry juice

1 c. ginger syrup, or to taste (recipe follows)

splash club soda

shaved ginger

DIRECTIONS:

For the ginger syrup:

- 4-in. piece ginger, peeled and roughly chopped
- ½ c. sugar
- 1-½ c. water

Place all syrup ingredients in a saucepan and simmer until sugar dissolves and the ginger is infused in the syrup, about 20 minutes.

Strain and allow to cool fully before use.

Bailey's Irish Cream

I remember growing up and watching the Waltons. On the TV show, there were two little old ladies who brewed bootleg whiskey they referred to as "The Recipe." One Christmas I made Joel a bottle of this and ever since he keeps asking me for another bottle of "The Recipe."

INGREDIENTS:

1-½ c. McMaster's® Canadian Whiskey

1 c. Eagle Brand® sweetened condensed milk

1 pint heavy whipping cream

2 eggs

4 T. Hershey®'s Syrup, chocolate

½ t. vanilla extract

4 T. water

DIRECTIONS:

Mix all ingredients in blender. Store in refrigerator.

Mix with coffee or just add ice to serve.

notes

soups and salads

Since Dad's retirement, he's been doing loads of cooking. One of his specialties is soup. And when Dad makes soup, he makes HUGE batches. In fact, the freezer is always filled with containers of soup. Anytime you visit, he'll send you home with soup. These next few recipes are some of his favorites.

Old-Fashioned Cabbage Soup

INGREDIENTS:

1/3 c. chopped onion
1/2 c. celery, sliced
1/4 c. margarine
1/2 c. flour
8 c. chicken broth
4 c. shredded cabbage (Dad uses more)
8–12 oz. fully cooked Polish sausage, halved lengthwise and thinly sliced
dash pepper
2 t. snipped parsley

DIRECTIONS:

In lg. soup pot or Dutch oven, sauté onion and celery in margarine until tender but not browned. Stir in flour until fully incorporated.

Stir in chicken broth. Add shredded cabbage. Cook and stir until soup has thickened and is bubbly. Reduce heat, simmer soup uncovered about 5 minutes.

Stir in sausage, pepper and parsley. Cook uncovered for 3 minutes more.

Makes 10 side dish servings or 6 main dish servings.

Hot Stuff Kielbasa-Cheese Soup

INGREDIENTS:

1 lg. onion, halved lengthwise and thinly sliced
1 c. sliced celery
¼ c. butter or margarine
¼ c. all-purpose flour
2 t. Worcestershire sauce
¾ t. dry mustard
1 can and 1 c. chicken broth
3 c. peeled and cubed potatoes or rutabaga
1 c. chopped carrots
8 oz. fully cooked kielbasa (Polish sausage), sliced in ¼–in. pieces
2-¼ c. milk
3 c. shredded sharp cheddar cheese
¼ t. coarsely ground pepper

DIRECTIONS:

In a 4-qt. Dutch oven, cook onion and celery in hot butter or margarine until tender.

Stir in flour, Worcestershire sauce and mustard; cook and stir for 2 minutes more. Carefully stir in broth.

Add potatoes, carrots and kielbasa. Bring to boiling. Reduce heat and simmer, covered, for about 20 minutes or until potatoes are tender.

Stir in milk. Heat and stir until mixture almost comes to a boil. Reduce heat.

Add 3 cups cheese and pepper; cook and stir till cheese is melted.

Ladle into soup bowls. Sprinkle with more cheese or pepper, if you like.

Serves 6 to 8.

Wild Rice Soup

Nobody can resist Dad's wild rice soup and NOTHING tastes better on a cold Minnesota night. Dad actually got this recipe from our very good family friend Shirley Scheidel.

INGREDIENTS:

1/3 c. uncooked wild rice
4 c. chicken stock
½ c. celery, diced
½ c. green pepper, chopped
½ c. onion, diced
½ c. fresh mushrooms, sliced
1 sm. carrot, shredded
1 clove garlic, minced
½ c. butter
½ c. flour
½ t. salt
¼ t. pepper
¼ t. curry powder
1 T. chopped pimento
¾ - 1 c. half-and-half (optional)
slivered almonds
½ c. cooked chicken or ham

DIRECTIONS:

Rinse wild rice with cold water; drain. Cook rice in chicken stock until tender.

In separate pan, cook and stir celery, green pepper, onion, mushrooms, carrots and garlic in butter until tender. Add flour and cook and stir 1–2 minutes.

Add chicken stock along with rice, ham or chicken, salt, pepper, curry powder and pimento. Mixture can be refrigerated at this point for later use.

To serve, heat soup, stir in half-and-half, checking for desired consistency.

Garnish with almonds.

Makes 6 servings.

notes

Beer Cheese Soup

Serving beer cheese soup is part of our Christmas Eve tradition. Dad labors over the soup, stirring it to the perfect consistency. He makes it ahead of time and puts it in a slow cooker or the microwave to reheat.

INGREDIENTS:

½ c. butter
1 c. flour
3 cans chicken broth
1 lb. Velveeta®, cubed
1 T. Worcestershire
6 oz. beer
½ c. onions, finely diced
1-½ c. evaporated milk
¼ t. yellow food coloring

DIRECTIONS:

Melt butter in a soup pot or Dutch oven.

Gradually add flour until smooth.

Gradually add broth until thick and smooth.

Add Velveeta® and remaining ingredients; heat on low and do not boil.

Broccoli-Leek Soup

These next two soup recipes come from Annie. She LOVES the fact that they are thick and creamy, even though they don't call for any cream.

INGREDIENTS:

2 T. olive oil
2 leeks, including tender green parts, finely chopped
1-½ lb. broccoli, trimmed, florets and stalks cut into 1-in. pieces
4 c. chicken broth
salt and white pepper

DIRECTIONS:

In a lg. saucepan over med. heat, warm the oil. Add the leeks and sauté until softened, 3–5 minutes. Add the broccoli and continue to sauté, stirring frequently until slightly softened, about 2 minutes longer.

Add the stock and bring to a simmer over med. heat. Cover partially and cook until the vegetables are tender when pierced with a sharp knife, 15–20 minutes. Remove from the heat.

In a blender or food processor, purée the soup in batches until smooth and return the soup to the pan. Reheat until warm.

Add salt and white pepper to taste.

Note: This is great with some cooked rice stirred in or topped with a little cheddar cheese.

Purée of Vegetable Soup

INGREDIENTS:

2 T. olive oil
3 leeks, including light green parts, finely chopped
4 carrots, peeled and sliced
4 zucchini, sliced
3 waxy potatoes (about 1 lb.), peeled and sliced
1-½ T. tomato paste
6 c. chicken stock
1 c. chickpeas, rinsed and drained
1 T. freshly squeezed lemon juice
salt and white pepper to taste

DIRECTIONS:

In a lg. saucepan over med. heat, warm the oil. Add the leeks and sauté until softened, about 5 minutes.

Add the carrots, zucchini and potatoes and sauté until they begin to soften, about 3 minutes.

Add the tomato paste and stock, cover partially and simmer until the vegetables are tender, 25–30 minutes.

Add the chickpeas and cook until heated through, about 3 minutes longer.

Stir in the lemon juice and salt and white pepper to taste. Remove the soup from the heat.

In a blender or food processor, purée the soup in batches until smooth and return the soup to the pan. Reheat until warm.

Serve alone or with a little shredded cheese and croutons.

Creamy Squash Soup

I made this for Thanksgiving 2007. We served soup and appetizers at noon. As the hostess, I was trying to clear the "snacks" away by 1:30 so we wouldn't ruin our 4:30 dinner. Of course, the family was giving me a lot of "heat" as I gave them the appetizer-clearing countdown. They didn't stay mad once they tasted this soup! It is very simple and really tasty!

INGREDIENTS:

2 lbs. butternut squash, halved, peeled, seeded and cut into 1-in. pieces

1-½ c. onions, diced

2 carrots, peeled and diced

3 14-¾-oz. cans chicken broth

½ t. salt

2 T. butter

½ c. light cream

sour cream for garnish

DIRECTIONS:

In a med. saucepan, combine squash, onion, carrots, broth and salt. Simmer uncovered until squash is very tender, about 20 minutes.

Purée soup in a blender or food processor with the butter. (I use my Bamix®!)

Whisk cream into soup.

Serve with a dollop of sour cream, if desired.

Refried Bean Soup

Melissa found this simple soup recipe. It is great because you can keep all the ingredients on hand and whip up dinner in no time. (With four kids, this is a priority.) One evening Melissa started dinner before her husband Joel got home from work. Kayla, their daughter, was serving the soup and she dished up seconds and maybe even thirds. When Joel arrived home, they were raving about the soup. He went to ladle himself a bowl full and all he found was an empty pot. I think Melissa started doubling the recipe after that night.

INGREDIENTS:

1 med. onion, chopped

1 green pepper, chopped

2 T. olive oil

1 can kidney beans, drained and rinsed

1 can black beans, drained and rinsed

1 can chicken broth

1 can Mexican-style stewed tomatoes

1 can fat-free refried beans

¼ t. cumin

2 t. minced garlic

DIRECTIONS:

Chop onion and green pepper and sauté in olive oil until tender.

Add the rest of the ingredients and stir and warm up for 5–7 minutes.

Simmer and serve.

Texas-Style Chili

On a snowy December day in 2005, I first discovered this recipe and I've been experimenting with it ever since. Add whatever you like…you really can't go wrong with chili!

INGREDIENTS:

3 lbs. ground beef
1 lb. bulk hot sausage
3 med. onions, chopped
4 cloves garlic, minced
¼ c. chili powder
2 T. flour
1 T. sugar
1 T. dried oregano
1 t. salt
2 28-oz. cans whole tomatoes, chopped, with their juice
3 16-oz. cans kidney beans or hot chili beans, drained
few dashes of Tabasco® sauce
pinch of dried red pepper flakes

OPTIONAL ADDITIONS:

cubed beef, chopped carrots, jalapeno peppers

DIRECTIONS:

Combine the ground beef, sausage, onions and garlic in a Dutch oven.

Cook over med. heat until the meat is browned; stir the meat to break it up as it cooks. Drain off the pan drippings.

Stir in chili powder, flour, sugar, oregano and salt and stir well to mix. Cover and simmer for an hour, stirring occasionally.

Add the tomatoes and beans and simmer for 20 minutes longer.

Sour Cream Cucumbers and Wilted Lettuce Salad

Dad's mom died when he was three years old, so his dad and his grandma Mary Nusser raised him. Sour cream cucumbers and wilted lettuce salad were two of Dad's favorite Grandma Nusser creations. When Mom married Dad, he wanted her to make these two salads. Unfortunately for Mom, Grandma Nusser didn't use many recipes. Mom says it took much trial and error to perfect these recipes. After forty-eight years, Dad will tell you that Mom has definitely mastered "sweated cukes" and wilted lettuce salad.

Sour Cream Cucumbers

INGREDIENTS:

2 lg. cucumbers, peeled and sliced thinly
1 lg. onion, sliced into rings
¾ c. sour cream
3 T. cider vinegar
2 T. sugar
salt and pepper to taste

DIRECTIONS:

In a bowl, combine cucumbers and onions.

Combine remaining ingredients and pour over cucumbers. Mix well and chill.

Wilted Lettuce Salad

INGREDIENTS:

3 bacon slices
2 T. vinegar
½ t. dry mustard
1 clove of garlic, minced (or garlic salt)
⅛ t. salt
⅛ t. pepper

DIRECTIONS:

Fry and dice bacon. Remove from pan and pour off all but 1–2 T. of bacon grease.

Add remaining ingredients to bacon grease.

Bring to a simmer, pour over lettuce, add bacon and mix to coat lettuce.

Note: We usually double or triple recipe.

BLT Salad

Annie makes the best salads. I think she takes after Great Grandma Nusser, however. In her words, "I just add stuff when I make salads. Use your judgment when adding the extras and don't go overboard on the dressing…I hate soggy salad." We asked her to invent some recipes and she came up with the next four salads.

INGREDIENTS:

romaine or the lettuce of your choice, washed and chopped

bacon, cut into 1-in. pieces and cooked until crispy

sunflower seeds

fancy croutons

shredded cheddar cheese

1 bottle Kraft® Tangy Tomato Salad Dressing

DIRECTIONS:

Put as much lettuce as you like in a lg. salad bowl.

Add sunflower seeds, croutons and bacon (about ⅛–¼ cup each per serving).

Toss with salad dressing right before serving.

Sprinkle the top with additional sunflower seeds.

Chinese Chicken Salad

INGREDIENTS:

romaine or the lettuce of your choice, washed and chopped

chow mein noodles

1–2 cans mandarin oranges, drained

chopped or shredded cooked chicken

toasted sliced almonds

Girard's® Chinese Chicken Salad Dressing

DIRECTIONS:

Put as much lettuce as you like in a lg. bowl.

Add chow mein noodles, oranges, chicken and almonds (about ⅛–¼ cup each per serving).

Toss salad with dressing right before serving.

Mexican Salad

While planning Ellie's First Communion/*Cinco de Mayo* party, Annie couldn't find a salad recipe that would work with her fajita/taco bar. She created this salad and it is one of our favorites.

INGREDIENTS:

romaine or lettuce of your choice, cleaned and chopped

1 can of corn, drained

1 can of black beans, drained

red and green peppers, finely chopped

shredded cheddar cheese

chopped or shredded cooked chicken (optional)

tortilla chips, broken up

DIRECTIONS:

Put lettuce in a serving bowl.

Add corn, beans, peppers and cheese. Toss with dressing (recipe follows).

Top with broken-up chips.

Dressing:

1 cup of your favorite salsa

1 cup of ranch dressing

Mix the two ingredients together until fully incorporated.

Poppy Seed and Cashew Salad

Annie is a custom home interior seamstress. In the summer of 2005, she traveled to Northfield to do some work for a client, Julie Pritchard. Julie is one of Annie's favorite clients because she always has a Diet Coke® waiting for her and she serves her a delicious lunch. Oh, and she never let's Annie get back on the road without another Diet Coke® and a bag of pretzels. We're just happy Annie didn't leave without this recipe!

INGREDIENTS:

romaine or the lettuce of your choice, washed and chopped

shredded Swiss cheese

salted cashews

1–2 Granny Smith apples, chopped

Craisins®

poppy seed dressing

DIRECTIONS:

Put as much lettuce as you like in a lg. salad bowl.

Add cheese, cashews, apples and Craisins® (about ⅛–¼ cup each per serving).

Toss salad with dressing right before serving.

Grandma's Jell-O® Applesauce Salad

Grandma Gina always brought some type of Jell-O creation for her great-grandkids, and this was one of their favorites.

INGREDIENTS:

1 lg. pkg. raspberry Jell-O®
2 c. boiling water
1 T. cinnamon candies
2 c. applesauce

DIRECTIONS:

Dissolve candies in a little warm water.
In another bowl, mix boiling water with contents of Jell-O® package.
Add dissolved candies and applesauce. Mix well.
Chill until set and serve.

Family Favorite Mandarin Orange Salad

No one is certain if this is a salad or a dessert!

INGREDIENTS:

2 sm. pkgs. orange Jell-O®
2 c. boiling water
2 sm. cans mandarin oranges
1 sm. container of Cool Whip® whipped topping

DIRECTIONS:

Dissolve Jell-O® in boiling water.
Drain juice from mandarin oranges and add juice to Jell-O®.
Chill until the mixture just begins to set. (As Mom says, "until it is squiggly")
Beat with container of Cool Whip.
Fold in mandarin oranges.

Chinese Cold Slaw

INGREDIENTS:

1 bag pre-chopped cabbage
Leeann Chin® Asian Salad Dressing
1 c. toasted sliced almonds

DIRECTIONS:

Put cabbage in a bowl.
Add about 1 c. of dressing. Stir so cabbage is covered, but not soggy. Add more dressing if necessary.
Top with toasted almonds.

Grandma Gina's Potato Salad

Grandma Gina made the BEST potato salad. We have so many wonderful memories of it. When Grandma turned seventy, we had a surprise party at the "Rad on Mad." To really throw her off, we asked her to make the potato salad for the event. It worked! She never guessed that the party was in her honor.

We always have two bowls of potato salad at large family gatherings: one with onions and the other without (for my Uncle Curt). Our traditional Christmas Eve meal includes beer cheese soup, hot beefs and potato salad. I remember one year Mom decided to make the potato salad. To save time, she mixed the dressing in advance. Now, refrigerator space is always at a premium, especially during the holidays; to make room for everything, Mom will often downsize original containers and place the contents in Tupperware. Well, on Christmas Eve I looked over at her and told her the potato salad tasted a little like nutmeg. She got the giggles and could hardly admit it, but then she said that, after boiling, peeling and cubing the potatoes, she had mistakenly grabbed the Tupperware filled with eggnog. Upon covering the potatoes in a holiday beverage, she tried to repair the error by "rinsing" them off. I could still taste it!

After Grandma died, nobody wanted to attempt this recipe. I hosted Christmas Eve a few years ago and thought I'd surprise the family by making Grandma's recipe. While *al dente* may be desirable for pasta, it just doesn't work for potatoes. And my potatoes were *al dente*. Even after all that work, I knew it was bad when nobody wanted any leftovers! I don't know if I'll ever try this again, but it certainly gave me a GREATER appreciation for the many hours Grandma spent making her potato salad.

INGREDIENTS:

5 cups diced, cooked potatoes

½ c. shopped onion

4-6 hard boiled eggs, chopped & sliced

Dressing (recipe follows)

Make Dressing and set aside.

Toss the potatoes, onions and eggs together. Coat with desired amount of dressing. Place in bowl and top with sliced eggs.

DRESSING:

½ c. sugar

⅓ c. vinegar

1 T. flour

1 t. salt

1 t. dry mustard

3 egg yolks or 2 whole eggs

Kraft Miracle Whip®

DIRECTIONS:

Beat the eggs yolks or whole eggs well.

Add the rest of ingredients; mix well.

Put mixture in a saucepan and cook until thick; stir all the while so that it does not scorch.

Mix equal parts of dressing with Miracle Whip®. If too thick, thin with cream or evaporated milk.

Add prepared mustard to taste.

Crispy Oriental Salad

Here are two recipes from Mom using the staple that every college kid has on hand, instant ramen noodles.

INGREDIENTS:

½ c. butter

2 t. sugar

½ c. sesame seeds or sunflower seeds

2 3-oz. pkgs. instant ramen noodles, uncooked and broken up (discard seasoning packet)

3 oz. sliced almonds

1 lg. head or 2 sm. heads bok choy (about 2 lb.)

4 green onions with tops, sliced

DIRECTIONS:

In a lg. skillet, melt butter.

Add sugar, sesame seeds, noodles and almonds.

Cook and stir until lightly browned, about 5 minutes. Cool to room temperature.

Coarsely chop bok choy, using both stalks and leaves. Add onions and chill.

When cool, toss greens with noodle mixture and dressing (recipe follows).

Dressing:

¾ c. vegetable oil

¼ c. red wine vinegar

½ c. sugar

2 T. soy sauce

Combine ingredients in a jar with a lid and shake well.

Ramen Noodle Coleslaw

INGREDIENTS:

½ c. oil
3 T. sugar
3 green onions, chopped
1 pkg. instant ramen noodles, crumbled
1 cabbage, shredded
1 carrot, shredded
1 green pepper (optional)

DIRECTIONS:

Mix oil, sugar and noodle seasoning. Set aside

Sauté noodles and slivered almonds in butter.

Toss cabbage, carrot and pepper with seasoning mixture, noodles and almonds just before serving.

notes

Spinach and Blue Cheese Salad with Sliced Apples and Spiced Caramelized Pecans

This is one of my FAVORITE salads. I debuted this recipe at Thanksgiving 2005. Not everybody in the family likes spinach or blue cheese; and you can omit them and substitute romaine, and it will still taste great.

INGREDIENTS:

1 apple, sliced

1 small lemon, juiced

8 oz. spinach, washed, thoroughly dried and stemmed

5 oz. blue cheese, crumbled

kosher salt and freshly ground white pepper

½ c. house dressing (recipe follows)

1-½ c. spiced caramelized pecans (recipe follows)

DIRECTIONS:

Sprinkle lemon juice over the apple slices.

Combine apple, spinach and blue cheese.

Season lightly with salt and pepper and toss with the dressing. Adjust seasoning to taste.

To serve, divide the salad among 4 plates and sprinkle with pecans.

House Dressing

2 lg. shallots, minced
1 T. Dijon mustard
2 T. zinfandel vinegar
2 T. sherry wine vinegar
½ c. olive oil
½ c. vegetable oil
salt and freshly ground white pepper

In a sm. bowl, whisk together the shallots and the mustard.
Whisk in the vinegars and then the olive and vegetable oils.
Season with salt and pepper to taste.
Transfer to a covered container and refrigerate until needed.

Spiced Caramelized Pecans

2 c. pecan halves
1 t. kosher salt
½ t. cayenne pepper
½ c. powdered sugar

Place nuts in a bowl and sprinkle with water.
Season with salt and cayenne pepper.
Add ⅓ c. powdered sugar. Toss to coat.
Pour mixture onto a baking sheet and bake at 350 degrees for 15–20 minutes, stirring every 5 minutes.

BBQ Chicken Chopped Salad

I absolutely love BBQ ANYTHING! I first made this for Easter 2002. Melissa even loved the leftovers that Joel delivered to her in the hospital. Their son Jack had just been born the day before!

INGREDIENTS:

Salad:

3–4 romaine hearts, rinsed, dried and cut into ⅛-in. strips

12 lg. fresh basil leaves, cut into ⅛-in. strips

2 c. shredded Monterey Jack cheese

1 c. canned black beans, rinsed and drained

1 c. canned sweet white corn, drained

2 lbs. ripe, fresh tomatoes diced into ½-in. pieces

½ c. BBQ sauce

¼ c. green onions, thinly sliced

tortilla strips or tortilla chips, crunched

DIRECTIONS:

In lg. mixing bowl, toss together the lettuce, basil, cheese, beans, corn, dressing (recipe follows) and some tortilla strips.

Transfer salads to serving plates.

Surround each salad with diced tomatoes and remaining tortilla strips.

Top each salad with BBQ chicken (recipe follows) and drizzle the chicken with extra BBQ sauce. Garnish with green onions.

Dressing:

½ t. dry mustard

¼ t. cold water

2-¾ c. mayonnaise

1 c. buttermilk

7 T. sour cream

2-½ T. apple cider vinegar

1-½ T. thinly sliced scallions

2 t. garlic, minced

1-½ t. Worcestershire sauce

1 t. dill

¼ t. oregano

Use a fork to stir together mustard and water, forming a paste. Set aside for 10 minutes.

Add all the remaining dressing ingredients to the bowl and, using a handheld mixer, blend together on low speed until smooth.

BBQ Chicken:

4 boneless, skinless chicken breasts, cooked and diced

¼ c. sweet and spicy BBQ sauce

Toss chicken with BBQ sauce.

Wild Rice Salad

Sometimes recipes are like your clothes. You put something in the back of your closet and you forget it. When we were talking about putting this book together, I told Melissa she had to submit this recipe. She must have put this recipe in the VERY back of her recipe box, because she couldn't remember preparing it. I'm hoping she'll dust it off and bring it out this summer. I have no doubt that it will still fit.

INGREDIENTS:

1 c. cooked wild rice

⅔ c. frozen peas

¼ c. green onions, chopped

4 hard boiled eggs, chopped

½ c. cheese, diced

DIRECTIONS:

Combine all ingredients.

Toss with dressing (recipe follows) and chill.

Dressing:

¼ c. brown sugar

½ t. salt

¼ t. pepper

⅓ c. mayonnaise

1-½ t. mustard

Whisk all ingredients together. Chill until ready to use.

notes

Spanish Style Chicken Salad

The summer after I moved into my house, Dad and Joel came over to help dig a drainage system. Actually the way Dad remembers it, Joel stopped over one day to check things out…it happened to be the day I left this salad for lunch. They loved it and I hope you will, too.

INGREDIENTS:

2 teaspoons Dijon mustard
¼ c. sherry vinegar
¼ c. olive oil
¼ c. vegetable oil
3 lbs. chicken breasts, poached and cubed
1 c. good quality blue cheese, crumbled
6 slices cooked bacon, crumbled
⅔ c. spiced caramelized pecans (recipe follows)
enough romaine lettuce to line plates

DIRECTIONS:

In a sm. bowl whisk together mustard, vinegar, olive oil and vegetable oil. Set aside

In lg. bowl combine chicken, cheese, bacon and pecans. Mix to combine.

Add dressing and mix to coat. Serve on a bed of romaine lettuce.

Spiced Caramelized Pecans

2 c. pecan halves
1 t. kosher salt
½ t. cayenne pepper
⅓ c. powdered sugar

Place pecans in a bowl and sprinkle with water.

Season with salt and cayenne pepper.

Add powdered sugar. Toss to coat.

Bake at 350 degrees for 15–20 minutes, stirring every 5 minutes.

notes

Balsamic Vinaigrette

On November 5, 2002, Medtronic hosted "Take Your Parents to Work" day. Mom and Dad came up the night before and I made baked spaghetti and served it with a salad topped with this balsamic vinaigrette. It is one of my favorites.

INGREDIENTS:

1 c. olive oil
¼ c. balsamic vinegar
1-½ T. sugar
2 lg. cloves garlic, crushed
1 t. salt
½ t. pepper

DIRECTIONS:

Combine all the ingredients in a jar with a tight-fitting lid and shake well. Let stand for at least ½ hour before using.

Garlic-Herb Croutons

I save all my old bread and put it in the freezer. Once I have a big stash, I thaw it out to make these fabulous croutons. They are my brother Joel's favorites. He always proclaims, "You made these with LOVE!"

INGREDIENTS:

2-⅔ sticks unsalted butter
2 cloves garlic, minced
2 t. basil
½ t. salt
½ t. cayenne pepper
1 loaf country-style white bread, cut into 1-in. cubes

DIRECTIONS:

Preheat oven to 225 degrees.

In a saucepan over med.-low heat, melt the butter. Remove from the heat and stir in the seasonings.

Put the bread cubes in a lg. mixing bowl. Add the seasoned butter and quickly toss to coat the cubes evenly.

Spread cubes on a baking sheet and bake until they are golden brown on the outside and crisp throughout, about 1 hour.

Store in an airtight container for up to two weeks.

Note: To test for doneness, cut or carefully bite into one of the larger croutons; its center should be completely dry and crisp.

main courses and sandwiches

Dad's BBQ Ribs

On Mother's Day each year, Dad makes his world-famous BBQ country style ribs. He labors over them for days, grilling, marinating and roasting. My brother, brother-in-law and I are responsible for all other aspects of the meal, and it's no small chore to keep the moms out of the kitchen. It is a wonderful tradition Dad started a number of years ago. Moms deserve a day off and it's fun for everybody to wait on them for a change.

Dad doesn't have a "recipe" for these famous Mother's Day country style ribs and I doubt very many of you have three days to prepare them. So in a pinch, use the recipe that follows. The beauty of this recipe? You can make as few or as many ribs as you like. The meat just falls off the bones!

INGREDIENTS:

pork ribs
your favorite BBQ sauce

DIRECTIONS:

Put some BBQ sauce on bottom of slow cooker.

Add pork ribs.

Slather on more sauce.

Continue to layer ribs and sauce.

Cook in the slow cooker on low for 6–8 hours.

Chicken or Turkey Casserole

This is one of Mom's classics. She can whip this up the night before any gathering for very easy entertaining.

INGREDIENTS:

1 7-oz. pkg. elbow macaroni (do not cook)

1 can cream of chicken soup

1 can cream of mushroom soup

½ lb. grated cheddar cheese

¼ c. diced onion (optional)

2 c. diced cooked chicken or turkey

2 c. milk (can substitute 1-½ c milk and ½ c. broth)

sliced water chestnuts (optional)

DIRECTIONS:

Preheat oven to 350 degrees.

Mix all together and pour in casserole.

Refrigerate overnight.

Bake for 1 hour.

notes

Quesadillas

This is another quick dinner Melissa often throws together for her family. She calls this her "go to" meal when she has leftover chicken.

INGREDIENTS:

2 T. unsalted butter
1½ lb. onions, sliced
1 t. sugar
1-½ t. salt
¼ t. red pepper flakes
8 6- to 7-in. tortillas
2-⅔ c. shredded Monterey Jack cheese
1 c. cooked roasted chicken, shredded into sm. pieces
2 t. lime zest
4 t. lime juice
5 T. chopped cilantro, divided
oil for grilling or sautéing

DIRECTIONS:

Melt butter in lg. heavy skillet set over med. heat. When hot, add onions and cook, stirring often, 1 minute.

Add sugar and salt and continue to cook, stirring, until onions are soft and well browned, 15–20 minutes. Remove from heat.

Stir in red pepper flakes. Set aside.

Place tortillas on work surface. Sprinkle ⅓ c. cheese over each tortilla.

Divide onions and spread evenly over cheese layer.

Top with shredded chicken.

Sprinkle ¼ t. lime zest and ½ t. lime juice over each tortilla.

Finally, sprinkle ½ T. cilantro over each.

Fold tortillas in half to form half moons.

Lightly coat a stove-top grill pan or lg. skillet with oil.

Place pan over med.-high heat and, when hot, add enough quesadillas to fit comfortably in single layer.

Cook until golden brown outside and cheese has melted inside, 2 minutes or less per side.

Remove, cover loosely with foil and finish cooking the rest.

With sharp knife, cut each cooked quesadilla into 2 equal triangles.

Garnish with remaining cilantro.

Favorite Meatballs

Ann says these are Paul's favorite meatballs. She usually quadruples this recipe so she can bag up a few meals to place in the freezer. In her words, "If I am going to go through the mess of hand-rolling meatballs, there better be more than one or two meals to show for my efforts."

INGREDIENTS:

1 lb. (hamburger) ground beef

½ c. dry bread crumbs

¼ c. milk

2 T. onion, finely chopped

1 t. salt

½ t. Worcestershire sauce

1 egg

DIRECTIONS:

Mix ingredients together and shape into twenty 1-½-in. balls.

Cook over med. heat, turning occasionally, until brown, about 20 minutes, or cook in an ungreased pan in a 400-degree oven for 20-25 minutes. Turn once while cooking.

notes

Chicken Lasagna

When I lived in Orlando, this was my roommate Tad's FAVORITE dish. I remember trying to save money, so I cooked a whole chicken; I swear I dirtied every pan we had in our kitchen. To further add to the experience, the humidity was horrid and I was sweating like crazy! I first made this recipe for the Blue Earth County Favorite Food Show when I was in 4-H. I got a blue ribbon!

INGREDIENTS:

8 oz. lasagna noodles
6 T. butter
1 c. chopped onions
½ c. green pepper, chopped
2 cans cream of chicken soup
⅔ c. milk
12 oz. mushrooms, sliced
1-½ c. cottage cheese
3 c. cooked chicken, diced
2 c. shredded cheddar cheese
2 c. shredded mozzarella cheese
½ c. Parmesan cheese, grated

DIRECTIONS:

Preheat oven to 350 degrees.

Cook lasagna noodles according to package instructions. Drain and set aside.

To make the mushroom sauce, sauté butter, onion and green pepper; add the soup, milk and mushrooms.

To make the cheese/chicken sauce, combine cottage cheese, chicken and cheeses.

In a greased 9x13-in. pan, layer noodles, chicken/cheese sauces and mushroom sauce. Make 3 layers, ending with the mushroom sauce.

Bake for 1 hour. Let stand a few minutes before cutting.

Pheasant Stroganoff

The Saturday before the fishing opener, there is a tournament on Madison Lake. On Friday night, Dad hosts a "Guys' Game Feed" at the "Rad on Mad." This is one of the recipes he always prepares.

INGREDIENTS:

1 c. white wine
3 pheasant breasts
lemon pepper
salt
1 onion, diced
2 cans Campbell's® Condensed Golden Mushroom Soup
1 c. sour cream

DIRECTIONS:

Preheat oven to 325 degrees.

Put pheasant in a roasting pan with the wine, onion and seasoning. Bake for 2 hours.

Remove pheasant and de-bone.

Put meat back in roaster; stir in soup.

Bake for another hour.

Stir in sour cream 15 minutes before serving.

Serve over egg noodles or wild rice.

Note: Three pheasant breasts serve 4–6 people.

notes

Mom's Stuffed Shells

INGREDIENTS:

1 box jumbo dried pasta shells, cooked according to package directions

Meat Filling:

1-½ lb. ground beef
1 med. onion, chopped
½ lb. mozzarella cheese, grated
1 t. salt
1 t. Italian seasoning
¼ t. pepper
¼ c. Pour-over sauce (recipe follows)

Pour-over sauce:

2 T. cooking oil
½ c. onion, chopped
1 garlic clove, minced
3 c. tomato juice
6 oz. tomato paste
2 T. chili sauce
1 t. salt
½ t. pepper
½ t. sugar

DIRECTIONS:

Preheat oven to 350 degrees.

To make the pour-over sauce, sauté onion and garlic in oil; add tomato juice, paste, chili sauce, sugar, salt and pepper. Simmer for 10 minutes and set aside.

Brown beef together with the onion and drain. Return to pan and add seasoning and cheese. Cook for 5 minutes.

Stir in ¼ c. pour-over sauce. Remove from heat.

Pour half of the pour-over sauce in a 3-qt. casserole dish.

Stuff shells with meat filling; arrange on top of sauce in casserole and top with remaining sauce.

Bake for 30 minutes.

Beef Enchiladas

I made these for a little St. Patty's Day fiesta in 1997 when one of my lifelong friends, Derek Ferley, and I lived on Summit Avenue. Upon tasting this, he proclaimed, "This is my favorite thing you've ever made!" That was quite a big statement, as he had sampled loads of my cooking!

INGREDIENTS:

1 lb. ground beef
1 med. onion, chopped
½ c. sour cream
1 c. shredded cheddar cheese
¼ t. pepper
⅓ c. chopped green bell pepper
⅔ c. water
1 T. chili powder
½ t. oregano
¼ t. cumin
2 whole green chiles, chopped
1 clove garlic, finely chopped
1 15-oz. can tomato sauce
8 6-in. corn tortillas
Toppings: shredded cheese, sour cream, chopped onions

DIRECTIONS:

Cook beef in skillet over med. heat for 8–10 minutes, stirring occasionally, until brown; drain.

Stir in onion, sour cream, cheese and pepper. Cover and set aside.

Heat bell pepper, water, chili powder, oregano, cumin, chiles, garlic and tomato sauce to boiling, stirring occasionally; reduce heat to low. Simmer uncovered 5 minutes. Pour into pie plate.

Dip each tortilla into sauce to coat both sides. Spoon about ¼ c. beef mixture onto each tortilla; roll tortilla around filling.

Place seam-side down in ungreased 11x7-in. baking dish. Pour remaining sauce over enchiladas.

Bake uncovered at 350 degrees for about 20 minutes.

Garnish with toppings.

Beer Can Chicken

This is one of Dad's favorite Sunday dinner meals at the "Rad on Mad." The kids love this chicken and we all hope for leftovers, as the chicken is always so moist. Dad has a pretty big grill, so he can usually make two at once. Dad obviously took after Grandma Nusser; he recited this recipe to me over the phone from memory. And then he chuckled, "Oh, everybody knows how to make beer can chicken."

INGREDIENTS:

1 whole chicken

1 can of beer

seasoning (Dad says, "Let your imagination rule!")

DIRECTIONS:

Drink ½ can of beer.

Season chicken, especially the cavity. Dad uses garlic salt, seasoned salt, Mrs. Dash® and poultry seasoning. He even places some seasoning in the beer that's in the beer can.

Put the chicken on top of the beer can. (Or as Dad says, "Put the butt on the can and set the legs on the grill and close grill lid.")

Grill on low to med. for about 1-½ to 2 hours. (Or as Dad says, "Two to three beers later, it will be done.")

Grandpa and Patrick grilling Beer Can Chicken.

Chicken in Wine Sauce

This is a super easy recipe that makes you look like a gourmet! I couldn't begin to count the number of dinner parties I've had at which I served this dish.

INGREDIENTS:

4 lg. skinless, boneless chicken breasts
6 oz. Swiss cheese slices
1 10-¾-oz. can condensed cream of chicken soup
¼ c. white wine (more if desired)
salt and pepper to taste
1 c. herb-flavored stuffing mix, crushed
4 T. (½ stick) butter, melted

DIRECTIONS:

Preheat oven to 350 degrees.
Place chicken breasts in a shallow buttered casserole dish.
Layer cheese on top.
Mix soup, wine, salt and pepper; pour over cheese.
Sprinkle stuffing mix on top and drizzle with melted butter.
Bake for 1-½ hours.
Serves 4

Mom's Oven Stew

INGREDIENTS:

1-½ lb. stew meat, cubed
2 c. carrots, coarsely chopped
2 c. potatoes, coarsely chopped
2 c. celery, coarsely chopped
1 c. onions, chopped
1 can green beans
3 T. tapioca
salt and pepper to taste
1 28-oz. can whole tomatoes

DIRECTIONS:

Place meat and vegetables in a casserole; sprinkle with tapioca, salt and pepper.
Pour tomatoes on top.
Bake at 250 degrees for 6 hours, 275 degrees for 5 hours, or 300 degrees for 4 hours.
Note: This recipe doubles nicely.

Chicken Neapolitan

This is a great make-ahead dinner recipe from Annie's family. Teresa Ripple prepared this for Annie right after Sam was born. Annie now uses it as her standard recipe for new moms or others in need of a meal.

INGREDIENTS:

1 egg
½ c. milk
2 T. olive oil
1 c. Italian seasoned bread crumbs
3 whole chicken breasts, skinned, halved, boned and pounded flat
6 lg., fresh mushrooms, cut into thick slices
6 slices mozzarella cheese
⅓ c. grated Parmesan cheese
1 jar of spaghetti sauce (we like Newman's Own® Marinara Sauce)

DIRECTIONS:

Heat over to 375 degrees.

Beat egg and milk together in med. bowl.

Heat oil in skillet over med. heat.

Place bread crumbs in separate bowl. Dip chicken breasts, one at a time, in egg mixture, then crumbs. Shake off excess crumbs.

Sauté chicken in skillet until brown. Transfer chicken to 13x9-in. baking dish; top with mushrooms and mozzarella cheese.

Combine tomato sauce and seasonings; pour over chicken.

Sprinkle with Parmesan cheese. (Chicken can be prepared ahead to this point and refrigerated).

Bake for 20–30 minutes. Serve with pasta or noodles and a green salad, if desired.

notes

Cabbage Rolls

This is one of Dad's favorite dinners and the recipe comes from our very good friend, Kay Heil.

INGREDIENTS:

1 head of cabbage
2 lbs. ground beef
½ c. onions, chopped
1 c. minute rice
2 eggs
1 t. salt
½ t. pepper
2 cans tomato soup
1 15-oz. can diced tomatoes

DIRECTIONS:

Preheat oven to 350 degrees.

Parboil individual cabbage leaves and cool.

Mix the beef, onions, rice, eggs salt and pepper together.

Roll into short cigar shapes.

Place one cigar shaped meat mixture into a cooled cabbage leaf.

Fold in sides and then roll up leaf to completely enclose filling.

Place seam-side down and place cabbage rolls in a 9x13-inch baking pan.

To make the sauce, combine soup and diced tomatoes.

Pour over cabbage rolls.

Cover with foil and bake for one and one half hours.

notes

Baked Lemon Chicken

When my friend Mark Howard visited from Florida, I decided to host a little dinner party. I asked my sister what I should use for a centerpiece and she suggested I use a live goldfish for our Asian-themed dinner. Well, we knew the party was over when the fish went belly up. Nobody told me I shouldn't use tap water!

INGREDIENTS:

4 skinless, boneless chicken breasts
1 egg white
1 t. water
¼ c. flour
1 t. baking soda
½ t. cayenne pepper
Chinese lemon sauce (recipe follows)
chopped green onions and lemon slices

DIRECTIONS:

Preheat oven to 450 degrees and spray a cookie sheet with cooking spray.

Cut breasts crosswise in half.

Mix egg white and water in bowl. Add chicken; turn chicken to coat. Let stand 10 minutes.

Remove chicken from egg mixture; discard egg mixture.

Mix flour, baking soda and cayenne in plastic bag. Add 1 chicken piece at a time. Seal bag and shake to coat chicken.

Place chicken pieces on cookie sheet; spray with cooking spray. Bake uncovered 20–25 min.

Let chicken stand 5 minutes; cut each piece crosswise into about 5 slices.

Pour Chinese lemon sauce over chicken.

Garnish with lemon slices and green onions.

Chinese Lemon Sauce:

⅓ c. chicken broth
¼ c. sugar
1-½ t. grated lemon peel
3 T. lemon juice
2 T. light corn syrup
2 T. rice vinegar
1 clove garlic, finely chopped
¼ t. salt
2 t. cornstarch

Heat broth, sugar, lemon peel, juice, syrup, vinegar, garlic and salt to boiling, stirring occasionally.

Mix cornstarch and cold water; stir into sauce.

Cook and stir for about 30 seconds or until thickened.

Serve warm. Can be refrigerated up to 2 weeks.

Flour Tortillas

This is Paul's mom's recipe. He always makes it with refried beans.

INGREDIENTS:

1 lb. all purpose flour

1 T. salt

6 T. vegetable shortening

1 cup hot water

DIRECTIONS:

Put flour and salt into a mixing bowl. Cut in vegetable shortening until the mixture resembles fine breadcrumbs.

Mix in the water gradually to form a soft, pliable dough.

Knead on a well-floured surface until smooth and no longer sticky. Cover with a damp tea towel.

Cut off about 3 T. of dough at a time, keeping the rest covered. Knead the piece into a ball. Roll the ball into a very thin circle with a rolling pin.

Cook for 10 seconds per side in a hot frying pan.

notes

Turkey-Artichoke Lasagna

Melissa and Joel's family really likes this recipe. If you like artichokes, it's a nice twist on traditional lasagna.

INGREDIENTS:

2 t. olive oil

½ c. onion, chopped

1 garlic clove, chopped

9 oz. ground turkey

4 c. tomato sauce

1-½ c. frozen artichoke hearts, thawed, drained and chopped

2 c. part-skim ricotta cheese

6 oz. part-skim mozzarella cheese, shredded

¼ c. grated Parmesan cheese

1 lg. egg, lightly beaten

2 T. chopped fresh parsley

7 oz. dry lasagna noodles (about 9 noodles), cooked according to package directions

DIRECTIONS:

Preheat oven to 350 degrees.

In lg. skillet, heat oil; add onions and garlic and sauté until onions are translucent, stirring occasionally, 3–4 minutes.

Add turkey and cook until lightly browned, 5–6 minutes, stirring frequently to break up meat.

Stir in tomato sauce and artichokes; simmer 10 minutes.

In med. bowl, combine cheeses, egg and parsley.

To assemble lasagna, spread one third of the sauce mixture in 13x9-in. baking pan. Top with 3 lasagna noodles; spread with one third of cheese mixture. Repeat layer with remaining ingredients.

Cover with foil and bake 30 minutes; remove foil and bake 10 minutes longer. Let stand 15 minutes before cutting.

Favorite Meatloaf

This is one of Paul's favorites, so Annie always makes two because they love meatloaf sandwiches.

INGREDIENTS:

1-½ lbs. ground beef

1 c. dry bread crumbs

1 egg

1 T. Worcestershire sauce

1-½ t. salt

½ t. dry mustard

¼ t. pepper

DIRECTIONS:

Preheat oven to 350 degrees.

Mix all ingredients together in a bowl.

Spread mixture in an ungreased loaf pan.

Bake uncovered until done, about 1-½ hours.

Enchilada Casserole

This may be the recipe that started this entire book. Remember when I told you at the beginning of the book about my co-workers requesting that I make a cookbook? They made that request shortly after I served this at a department "Thank God He's a Country Boy" shower for Amy Draxten (Peterson). All the guests showed up in bad bridesmaids dresses and we had quite a get-up for Amy! (Veiled cowboy hat and silver boots included!)

INGREDIENTS:

2 lbs. lean ground beef
1 med. onion, chopped
2/3 c. water
1 1-1/4-oz. pkg taco seasoning
1 15-oz. can pinto beans, drained
1 15-1/4-oz. can corn, drained
1 4-oz. can chopped green chiles
1 14-1/2-oz. can petite diced tomatoes, undrained
1 19-oz. can enchilada sauce
20 6-in. corn tortillas
2 8-oz. pkgs. shredded Colby and Monterey Jack cheese

DIRECTIONS:

Preheat oven to 350 degrees and lightly grease a 13x9x2-in. baking dish.

In a lg. skillet, cook ground beef and onion over med. heat until meat is browned and crumbles; drain.

Add 2/3 c. water and taco seasoning; cook over med. heat for 10 minutes, stirring occasionally.

Stir in beans, corn, chiles, tomatoes and enchilada sauce. Remove from heat.

Tear corn tortillas into bite-size pieces. Place half of the tortillas into bottom of prepared baking dish. Spoon half of the meat mixture evenly over tortillas. Sprinkle with half of cheese. Repeat layers.

Bake for 30–40 minutes, or until hot and bubbly.

Hot Beefs

My Mom and Dad taught us how to entertain for crowds…it's not unusual to have over fifty guests to feed at the "Rad on Mad." They ALWAYS supply the sandwiches and these are a crowd favorite. They can be made and frozen in advance; just warm them up in a slow cooker. When you're serving these sandwiches, don't be stingy with the meat!

INGREDIENTS:

7 lbs. rump or sirloin tip
1 pkg. dry onion soup mix
4 beef bouillon cubes
salt and pepper
1 c. water

DIRECTIONS:

Preheat oven to 275 degrees.

Put meat in covered roasting pan with dry onion soup mix, bouillon cubes and water. Roast for 4 ½ hours.

Remove from oven, slice beef thin and put back in roaster; add salt and pepper to taste. Bake another 1-½ hours covered.

Shred beef; serve in buns.

Kayla, Josie and Ellie hanging out at the "Rad on Mad"

Turkey Sandwiches

This recipe comes from another good family friend, Marie Trautman.

INGREDIENTS:

1 20-lb. turkey
celery and onions (loads of them!)
water
1 stick of butter
5–6 chicken bouillon cubes
salt and pepper

DIRECTIONS:

Preheat oven to 325 degrees.

Rub inside of turkey with salt.

Chop celery and onions; cut small enough pieces to fit LOADS of it in the turkey.

Stuff the turkey cavity full.

Place turkey in roasting pan and cover the bottom of a roasting pan with water.

Place stick of butter in roasting pan.

Roast turkey. (Roast according to directions on turkey packaging.)

When well done, de-bone the turkey and discard the bones, leaving turkey in roasting pan with onion and celery.

Add bouillon cubes and season with salt and pepper.

Return to oven and heat until bouillon cubes dissolve and turkey is moist and well seasoned.

Fill buns with turkey meat...don't be stingy with the meat!!

Barbeque Pork Sandwich

INGREDIENTS:

6–8 lb. pork roast
1-½ c. onion, chopped
1 ½ c. celery, chopped
¾ c. barbeque sauce
1-½ c. catsup
salt and pepper
liquid smoke

DIRECTIONS:

Roast pork until very tender.

Pull off bone and discard bone.

Shred pork in roasting pan.

Mix the rest of the ingredients in a bowl and pour over pork.

Simmer for 1-2 hours.

Grandma Gina's Spoonburgers

INGREDIENTS:

1 lb. ground beef
2 T. oil
2/3 c. onions, chopped
1 T. prepared mustard
1 T. catsup
1 t. salt
1/8 tsp. pepper
1 can chicken gumbo soup, undiluted
1/4 c. water

DIRECTIONS:

Sauté meat for 10 minutes.

Drain grease and return to pan.

Add remaining ingredients and bring to boil. Lower heat and cook slowly for 30 minutes.

Spoon mixture onto buns and serve.

Maggie's Crumble Burgers

One of the first jobs Joel, Annie and I had was hoeing beans for Maggie and Dick Oberle. For those of you unfamiliar to this summer job, we basically walked between the rows of soybeans and hoed out the weeds. Our favorites were the big milkweed plants! This was not your average bean-hoeing job, as each day Maggie made us a home-cooked lunch. We'd take a break in their air-conditioned home and have these favorite crumble burgers for lunch. Joel also remembers the Kool-Aid® made with well water.

INGREDIENTS:

2 lbs. ground beef
1 can Campbell's® onion soup
2 T. flour

DIRECTIONS:

Brown hamburger; season with salt and pepper. Add soup and flour. Add water if needed. Heat and serve on buns.

Annie's Stromboli

I love this dish. There is just something wonderful about soft bread and melted cheese. When Annie serves these, she makes a variety of them the night before and then bakes them when the guests arrive. We had a surprise seventieth birthday party for Mom and Dad and I told Annie that I didn't think we needed them. Thank goodness she insisted, because without them we would have run out of food!

INGREDIENTS:

1 loaf frozen bread dough, thawed, or 1 Pillsbury® bread loaf

¼ - ½ lb. sliced meat (your choice)

¼ - ½ lb. sliced cheese (your choice)

cheese spreads or flavored cream cheese (your choice)

1 sm. jar roasted red peppers (optional)

anything else you like layered on a sandwich

DIRECTIONS:

Preheat oven to 350 degrees.

Roll out the bread dough onto a lightly floured surface into a rectangle about ¼ in. thick. If you are using the canned bread loaf, unroll it onto a lightly breaded surface.

Layer the meat, cheese and extas on the dough within an inch of the edges. If you are using spreadable cheese as a layer, spread that first.

Once you have everything layered, roll the dough. Gently press edges to seal and fold ends under. (If you are making this a day ahead, stop here and wrap the loaf in plastic wrap and refrigerate.)

Place loaf on a greased cookie sheet. With a sharp knife, cut 5 or 6 diagonal slices into the top of the loaf. Bake at 350 degrees for 25–30 minutes or until the edges are golden brown.

Let cool for a few minutes before cutting.

Note: You can also do a meatless version for your vegetarian friends.

Creamed Corn Casserole

No family holiday is complete without this creamed corn casserole. When I planned to host Easter one year, I actually considered omitting this starch from our menu. Lo and behold, Mom and Dad packed all the ingredients and put it together when they arrived.

INGREDIENTS:

½ c. onion, chopped
½ c. green pepper, chopped
½ c. butter
1 15-oz. can cream style corn
1 15-oz. can whole kernel corn, drained
3 eggs, slightly beaten
8-½ oz. corn muffin mix
8 oz. sour cream
1 can chopped green chiles
4 oz. (1-¼ c.) cheddar cheese, shredded

DIRECTIONS:

Preheat oven to 350 degrees.

Sauté onion, green pepper and butter in a pan.

Mix together all ingredients and put in 3-qt. casserole dish.

Bake for 45 minutes or until inserted knife comes out clean.

Roasted Vegetables Parmesan

At some point, we thought it would be wise to have some healthy side dishes at holidays. Unfortunately, none of them ever taste as good as the ones slathered in soup, covered in cheese and sprinkled with crumbled Ritz crackers…that is, until Melissa brought her roasted veggies.

INGREDIENTS:

2 med. zucchini, cut into 1-in. chunks

1 med. onion, cut into 8 wedges

1 med. sweet red bell pepper, seeded and cut into 1-in. chunks

8 oz. mushrooms, sliced, with stems removed

1 c. whole baby carrots

1 c. broccoli florets, sliced into ½ in. pieces

1 c. cauliflower florets, sliced into ½ in. pieces

1 bunch lg. asparagus, sliced into 1-in. segments

2 T. olive oil

½ t. salt

1 15-oz. can garbanzo beans (chick peas), drained and rinsed

1 14-½-oz. can diced tomatoes with garlic and Italian herbs

1 c. shredded Parmesan cheese

DIRECTIONS:

Preheat oven to 500 degrees.

In lg. mixing bowl, combine zucchini, onion, sweet bell pepper, mushrooms, carrots and asparagus. Drizzle with olive oil. Toss to coat.

Spread tossed vegetables evenly in lg. roasting pan or glass baking dish. Sprinkle with salt.

Roast vegetables uncovered for 15 minutes or until they begin to soften slightly.

Remove from oven and reduce oven temperature to 375 degrees.

Stir in garbanzo beans and diced tomatoes to vegetable mixture. Spread evenly. Roast uncovered for 10–12 minutes more, until heated through.

Sprinkle with Parmesan cheese and serve.

Roasted Asparagus

Mom and Dad brought this recipe back after they visited Aunt Helen and Uncle Delt in Florida. Aunt Helen is a great cook. This is my favorite way to eat asparagus.

INGREDIENTS:

2 lbs. fresh asparagus
olive oil
1-¼ t. kosher salt
pepper

DIRECTIONS:

Preheat oven to 400 degrees.

Break off the tough ends of the asparagus and. If the remaining stalks are thick, peel them.

Place the asparagus on a baking sheet, drizzle with olive oil, then roll to coat completely.

Spread the asparagus in a single layer and sprinkle liberally with salt and pepper.

Roast the asparagus for 15 to 20 minutes, until tender but still crisp.

Creamed Spinach

One night Melissa and Josie made this recipe and ended up eating the entire batch.

INGREDIENTS:

2 10-oz. bags spinach, stems removed
1 T. unsalted butter
1 T. flour
1 c. half and half
⅛ t. nutmeg
½ c. fresh grated Parmesan cheese
salt
pepper

DIRECTIONS:

Wash spinach in lukewarm water. Lift out of sink; do not spin.

Put in lg. bowl.

Put ½ of the spinach in lg. saucepan.

Cover and cook over med. heat, stirring often, for about 5 minutes.

Add the rest; drain in colander and rinse with cold water.

Squeeze a handful of spinach at a time to extract water and set aside.

Melt butter over low heat and add flour, whisking to incorporate. Let the mixture bubble but not brown for 1 minute.

Whisk in half and half and simmer over med. heat.

Cook until thick, about 3 minutes.

Stir in spinach and nutmeg, cook until heated, about 3 minutes.

Stir in cheese, salt and pepper and serve hot.

Wild Rice Dressing

Thank goodness Annie always makes a double batch of this…the leftovers are fantastic. Mom always tells stories about growing up and sharing holidays with Bens O'Hare. Bens used to love the crusty, crunchy parts of this dressing. In order to be certain the kitchen crew would get some, she would hide a bowl before they served their guests.

INGREDIENTS:

1 lb. ground beef
½ lb. pork sausage
½ c. onion, chopped
1 c. celery, chopped
½ c. butter
⅓ c. wild rice, uncooked
2 c. cold water
1 loaf of bread, cubed
1 T. poultry seasoning
salt and pepper to taste
1 can chicken broth or 8. oz. hot water

DIRECTIONS:

Brown ground beef and pork sausage; drain.

Sauté onions and celery in butter.

In a saucepan, combine wild rice with water. Bring to a boil for 1 minute. Cover and simmer for 45 minutes, until rice is tender and pops open. Rinse and drain rice.

Combine all ingredients and mix well, using chicken broth to moisten. You can use this as a stuffing for chicken, turkey or pork chops, or bake it on it's own at 350 degrees for 45 minutes to an hour.

notes

Holiday Cauliflower

I made this for the Easter 2005 holiday at my house. It was yummy. During the egg hunt, the Easter Bunny made a special appearance. (The Easter Bunny was played by my high school neighbor, Danny Morris.)

INGREDIENTS:

1 lg. head cauliflower
½ lb. fresh mushrooms, sliced
¼ c. green pepper, diced
¼ c. butter
⅓ c. flour
2 c. milk
1 t. salt
1 c. Swiss cheese, shredded

DIRECTIONS:

Preheat oven to 325 degrees.

Cut cauliflower into med.-sized florets; cook in boiling water until tender but crisp, about 10 minutes. Drain well; set aside.

In 2-qt. saucepan, sauté mushrooms and green pepper in butter until tender. Blend in flour. Gradually stir in milk. Cook, stirring constantly, over med. heat until mixture is thick. Add salt and cheese.

Place half of the cauliflower in buttered 2-qt. casserole dish. Cover with half of the sauce. Repeat layers.

Bake for 15 minutes.

Serves 8.

Overnight Wild Rice

Dad got this recipe from a very special lady, Muggs Schulze. He swears it is the ONLY way to cook wild rice!

INGREDIENTS:

2 c. wild rice, uncooked

5 c. boiling water

1 pkg. Lipton® Onion Soup Mix

1 t. salt

DIRECTIONS:

Preheat oven to 500 degrees.

Mix all the ingredients in a roasting pan. Cover and put in the hot oven for 15–20 minutes. Turn off the oven.

Leave in the oven overnight. Dad says, "Don't peek!"

In the morning, fluff with a fork.

Wild Rice Baron

INGREDIENTS:

2 c. wild rice (prepared as above)

1 lb. fresh mushrooms, sliced

½ c. chopped celery

1 c. chopped onion

½ c. slivered almonds, browned in butter

2 c. sour cream

¼ c. or less soy sauce (optional)

2 t. salt

¼ t. pepper

DIRECTIONS:

Sauté mushrooms, celery and onion in butter for 5–10 minutes.

Combine soy sauce, sour cream, salt, pepper, sautéed mixture and almonds. Add cooked wild rice. Toss lightly.

Place in a lightly buttered 3-qt. casserole. Bake uncovered in a 350-degree oven for about 1 hour.

Add more water if needed and season to taste. Stir several times.

Serve piping hot. Enjoy!

Note: Leftovers freeze and keep well.

Balsamic Grilled Vegetables

In September of 2005, I made these alongside a juicy steak when I was trying to impress a date. I called home to ask Dad how to season the steak. Fred and Kathy Bruckbauer were visiting Mom and Dad at the time and they had LOADS of "cooking" tips! Fred told me to use plenty of garlic…especially behind my ears!

INGREDIENTS:

1 med. yellow squash, sliced on the bias
1 med. zucchini, sliced on the bias
1 red onion, sliced in ½-in. circles
1 red bell pepper, stemmed, seeded and quartered
1 yellow bell pepper, stemmed, seeded and quartered
2 Portobello mushroom caps, grilled and peeled
3 green onions
kosher salt
freshly ground black pepper
½ c. olive oil
½ c. balsamic vinegar

DIRECTIONS:

Preheat grill to high.

Prepare all vegetables and place them in a plastic bag.

Season vegetables generously with salt and pepper and toss them in the bag with the olive oil and balsamic vinegar.

Place vegetables in grill basket on top of grill. Cook for a few minutes and toss. Grill until tender and are nicely marked by the grill.

Remove from grill and toss with an additional ¼ c. balsamic vinegar. Season with salt and pepper to taste.

Melissa's Cumin Cauliflower

INGREDIENTS:

1 lg. head cauliflower, about 2-¾ lbs
2–3 T. extra virgin olive oil
¼ c. ground cumin
salt and pepper

DIRECTIONS:

Preheat oven to 425 degrees.

Remove core from cauliflower. Break head into sm. florets, about ¾-in. wide.

Place in a lg. bowl and toss with olive oil. Sprinkle with salt and pepper to taste and toss with cumin.

Place in a rimmed baking sheet. Roast in oven for 30 minutes or until soft and caramelized, turning once during cooking.

Sprinkle with salt and pepper, if desired. Serve hot or at room temperature.

Annie's Cajun Yams

Annie and Paul purchased a Cajun cookbook during a 1997 trip to New Orleans. This recipe became an instant Thanksgiving classic. We now fight over who can bring this dish, because you know you'll receive loads of "ego biscuits" when it is served! It tastes more like a dessert! You'll be fighting over the leftovers.

INGREDIENTS:

2–3 boiled fresh yams, mashed with a fork, or 3 c. canned yams

½ c. sugar

2 eggs, beaten

1 t. salt

2 T. butter

⅛ t. cinnamon

½ t. nutmeg

½ c. evaporated milk

½ t. vanilla extract

topping (recipe follows)

DIRECTIONS:

Preheat oven to 350 degrees.

Combine mashed yams with all ingredients. Pour into greased dish and pat down.

Spread topping (recipe follows) over yam mixture; cover and bake for 40 minutes.

Serves 8.

Note: The yams will be sugary hot, so be careful when eating.

Topping:

½ c. brown sugar

⅓ c. flour

1 c. pecans, chopped

¼ c. butter, melted

Combine topping ingredients in a sm. bowl until well blended.

Topping will be a bit dry and will need to be broken up with your fingers; distribute evenly over yam mixture. Keep topping about ½ in. from the sides of the dish to prevent sticking.

Saucy Baked Beans

I debuted this recipe at the lake in the summer of 2006. The dish has been a hit at every BBQ since!

INGREDIENTS:

2 42-oz. cans pork and beans, drained
10 oz. BBQ pork (packaged in tub)
1 med. onion, chopped
½ c. chili sauce
¼ c. brown sugar, firmly packed
¼ c. dark corn syrup
2 T. liquid smoke
2 T. mustard

DIRECTIONS:

Preheat oven to 350 degrees.
Lightly grease a 13x9x2-in. baking dish.
In a lg. bowl, combine all ingredients. Spoon into prepared baking dish.
Bake 45–50 minutes, or until hot and bubbly.

notes

Hashbrowns Deluxe

Nothing goes better with a holiday ham than Mom's hashbrowns deluxe. Over the years, I've tried different types of cheesie potatoes, but I'm not sure why I bother. These are simply the best. And they're very easy to make.

INGREDIENTS:

2 lbs. frozen hash browns
½ c. melted butter
1 t. salt
1 onion, chopped
1 can cream of chicken soup
2 c. shredded cheddar cheese
1 12-oz. package sour cream (with chives)
2 c. cornflakes, crushed

DIRECTIONS:

Preheat oven to 350 degrees.
Mix all ingredients (except cornflakes and melted butter together) and put into 9x13-in. pan
Top with cornflakes and melted butter
Bake for 45–60 minutes.

Fresh Cranberry Relish

I hosted Thanksgiving 2006 and these were a HIT! I think it was the only time people asked for seconds of the cranberries!

INGREDIENTS:

2 lbs. fresh cranberries
¾ c. sugar
¼ c. Grand Marnier® liqueur
1 orange, zested and juiced

DIRECTIONS:

Place all the ingredients in the bowl of a food processor; pulse several times to break down the cranberries and incorporate the ingredients; it should still be a bit chunky. (I use my Bamix® for this!)
Allow the cranberry relish to sit at room temperature for at least 30 minutes, so the flavors can marry.

brunch and breads

Baked French Toast

This is one of our favorite breakfast treats. The recipe comes from a very good family friend, Alice Hermer. Sunday mornings at the lake are always busy with trying to get everybody up, showered, fed and on their way to church. Late on Saturday evening, somebody can always be found in the kitchen putting together something for Sunday's breakfast.

INGREDIENTS:

1 stick butter
1-½ c. milk
6 eggs
1 c. brown sugar
1 loaf French bread
1 t. cinnamon

DIRECTIONS:

Combine melted butter, brown sugar and cinnamon and spread out on bottom of 9-x-13-in. pan.

Slice French bread in 1-in. pieces. Make 2 layers over the brown sugar bottom.

Beat eggs and milk. Pour over bread. Cover and refrigerate overnight.

Bake uncovered for 30 minutes in 350-degree oven.

Egg Bake

When Annie and Paul got married, we held their traditional gift opening at the house. Mom and Dad were so well prepared they had given neighbors and friends all the ingredients, bagged and ready for assembly. What a smart way to entertain.

INGREDIENTS:

8 slices day-old bread, grated
2 c. diced baked ham
4 T. onion, minced
3 T. flour
3 c. grated cheddar cheese
2 T. yellow mustard
8 eggs
2-½ c. milk
garlic salt (optional)

DIRECTIONS:

Butter a 9x13-in. pan. Put in grated bread; sprinkle on ham and onion and top with cheese.

Beat together remaining ingredients and pour over cheese. Refrigerate overnight.

Bake at 350 degrees for 60 minutes. Let stand for 5–10 minutes before serving.

notes

Tortilla Egg Bake

The first time I made this was for a little reunion with my friend Kim (Rabehl) Kainz and her family in July 2005. Kim and I first met when we were state 4-H ambassadors. If Kim would have been judging, I have no doubt that I would have received a blue ribbon! :)

INGREDIENTS:

12 oz. Jimmy Dean® sausage
⅔ c. onions, chopped
⅓ c. green pepper, chopped
12 6-in. corn tortillas
2-½ c. Colby Jack cheese, grated
2 c. milk
4 eggs, beaten
½ t. salt
⅛ t. pepper
½ c. tomato sauce
1 4-oz. can diced green chiles

DIRECTIONS:

Cook sausage, onions and green peppers.
Beat together eggs, milk, salt, pepper, tomato sauce and chiles.
In 9x13-in. glass baking dish, layer corn tortillas, ½ of meat mixture and ½ of cheese. Repeat with corn tortillas, meat and cheese.
Pour milk, eggs, tomato sauce and chili mixture on top. Refrigerate overnight.
Bake at 325 degrees for 45 minutes to 1 hour, until heated throughout.
Serve with salsa and sour cream.

Frozen Fruit Slush

INGREDIENTS:

1 6 oz. container frozen orange juice
1 6-oz. container frozen lemonade
1 10-oz. container frozen strawberries
1 4-oz. jar maraschino cherries, with juice
3–4 bananas, diced
1 16-oz. can crushed pineapple, with juice
¾ c. sugar
3 c. water

DIRECTIONS:

Mix juices and strawberries in lg. bowl.
Add fruits with juices, sugar and water.
Freeze in serving containers.
Remove from freezer ½ hour before serving. Serve in slushy state.

Sticky Buns

INGREDIENTS:

1 pkg. frozen rolls (24)

1 sm. pkg. butterscotch pudding mix (not instant)

1 c. brown sugar

1 tsp. cinnamon

½ c. margarine (melted)

½ c. pecans, chopped

DIRECTIONS:

Generously butter a Bundt pan and sprinkle nuts into bottom of pan.

Place rolls on top of nuts.

Combine pudding, sugar and cinnamon, and sprinkle over rolls.

Pour melted margarine over top of rolls and let rise overnight. Put waxed paper or a light cloth over the pan and keep out of drafts.

Bake at 350 degrees for 30 minutes.

Let cool and invert on plate to serve.

notes

Breakfast Bundle

Kayla is the oldest grandchild and she has become quite the cook. This is one of her creations…it's very impressive!

INGREDIENTS:

1 box puff pastry dough (1.1 lb.)
2 T. unsalted butter
1 c. frozen, cubed hash brown potatoes
1 c. red or green bell peppers, seeded and diced
½ c. onion, diced
1 c. smoked ham, diced
11 eggs
2 T. minced fresh chives
4 oz. cream cheese, softened
2 T. orange juice
1 egg
1 T. water
2 T. parmesan cheese, shredded

DIRECTIONS:

Preheat oven to 450 degrees.

Melt butter in a lg. nonstick skillet over med.-high heat. Add potatoes and sauté 5 minutes. Stir in bell peppers and onion; sauté 3 minutes, then add ham.

Whisk eggs and chives together. Add them to the pan and scramble just until set. Season with salt and pepper. Remove from heat.

Stir in cream cheese and juice until blended. Refrigerate eggs while rolling the pastry sheet.

Unfold a pastry sheet on a work surface that has been lightly dusted with flour. Roll pastry to 12x10 in. then transfer to a piece of parchment cut to fit a baking sheet. Cut off the top corners of the pastry. Create 3-in. long strips by cutting pastry dough at a 45 degree angle every 1". When you get to the bottom stip, cut it off to create an inverted triangle. Place ½ of the egg mixture down the center of the pastry. Fold up the flaps at both ends, then braid the strips across the filling. Repeat with remaining pastry and egg filling. Transfer parchment and strudels to baking sheets.

Combine the remaining egg and water; brush over top of strudels and sprinkle with cheese. (At this point, strudels may be wrapped in plastic and chilled overnight.)

Bake strudels for 20–30 minutes, or until golden. Let cool 5 minutes before slicing.

Tofu 'n' Carrot Muffins

This is one of Kayla's favorite recipes. Melissa says, "The kids love to eat these and they don't even know they are so healthy."

INGREDIENTS:

2 eggs
1 c. honey
½ c. safflower oil
1 10-½-oz. package tofu, drained
2 t. baking soda
1 t. ground cinnamon
1 t. ground nutmeg
¼ t. salt
1 T. vanilla extract
2 c. whole wheat flour
1 c. carrots, shredded
½ c. dates or raisins, chopped
powdered sugar for dusting

DIRECTIONS:

Preheat oven to 325 degrees.

In blender container or food processor bowl, combine eggs, honey, oil, tofu, cinnamon, nutmeg, salt and vanilla; blend until smooth.

Pour mixture into a bowl; blend in flour, carrots, and dates.

Spoon batter into paper-lined muffin pans. Bake until muffins test down with a wooden pick (17–20 minutes).

Remove to wire rack to cool.

When cool, dust lightly with powdered sugar.

Store covered in refrigerator.

Makes about 1-½ dozen.

Little Cinnamon Muffins

These are the BEST! They will remind you of the mini-doughnut stand at the MN State Fair. I first made them for a Palm Sunday brunch I held for some girlfriends. Before brunch, we went to my church, St. Joan of Arc, and heard Robby Robinson perform. It was a perfect Sunday!

INGREDIENTS:

5 T. butter
½ c. sugar
1 egg
1-½ c. flour
1-½ t. baking powder
¼ t. salt
½ t. nutmeg
½ c. milk
¼ lb. butter, melted
½ c. sugar
1 T. cinnamon

DIRECTIONS:

Preheat oven to 400 degrees.

Cream butter and sugar; add egg and beat again.

Mix dry ingredients together and add to butter mixture. Add milk.

Pour into greased miniature muffin tins.

Bake for 10–15 minutes or until lightly browned.

Combine sugar and cinnamon.

Dip each muffin into melted butter and roll in cinnamon-sugar mixture.

Makes 36 sm. muffins.

Annie's Kringle

It wouldn't be Christmas without Annie's famous kringle. I guess Mom started making this recipe when she hosted bridge club and baby or bridal showers, but now it is definitely Annie's specialty. Annie's brother-in-law, Steve Ripple, requests this every year for their Christmas Eve celebration. Now she makes two so he can take one home…I'll bet it is one of his favorite presents each year.

INGREDIENTS:

Crust
- 1 c. flour
- ½ c. butter
- 1 T. water

Mix all ingredients together to form a piecrust.

Divide in half and form into two circles on a lg. parchment-lined cookie sheet. (I actually make one lg. circle and use my serving plate to determine circle size. I will even trace the plate onto the parchment for a perfect fit.)

Filling
- 1 c. water
- ½ c. butter
- 1 c. flour
- 4 eggs
- 1 t. almond extract

DIRECTIONS:

Preheat oven to 250 degrees.

Heat water and butter to boiling: add all of the flour and stir vigorously over low heat until mixture forms a ball. Remove from heat.

Beat in eggs, one at a time. Add almond extract and spread mixture evenly over pastry crust.

Bake for 45–55 minutes.

Cool slightly and frost.

Frosting
- 1 c. powdered sugar
- 1 T. butter
- ½ t. almond extract
- milk or half-and-half
- slivered almonds

Combine powdered sugar, butter and almond flavoring.

Add milk and stir until it reaches a spreadable consistency.

Spread on kringle and top with almonds.

Mom's Banana Bread

INGREDIENTS:

½ c. vegetable shortening
1 c. sugar
2 eggs
2 lg. bananas, mashed (about 2 c.)
⅓ c. sour cream
2 c. flour
1 t. baking soda
½ t. salt

DIRECTIONS:

Preheat oven to 325 degrees.

Cream shortening, sugar and eggs.

Add mashed bananas and sour cream. Mix well.

Add dry ingredients and stir to incorporate.

Put into 1 lg. loaf pan or 2 sm. greased loaf pans.

Bake for 1 hour. (Less time is required for smaller pans.)

notes

Mom's Pumpkin Bread

INGREDIENTS:

2-½ c. sugar
scant c. cooking oil
4 eggs
1 15-oz. can pumpkin
3-½ c. flour
½ t. baking powder
2 t. baking soda
1-½ t. salt
1 t. EACH of the following spices:
- cloves
- cinnamon
- nutmeg
- allspice

⅓ c. water
⅓ c. molasses
1 c. raisins and nuts (optional)

DIRECTIONS:

Preheat oven to 350 degrees.

Sift spices with the flour.

In another bowl, mix sugar and oil.

Add eggs, pumpkin, water and molasses to sugar and oil mixture. Stir in spices and flour. Mix well.

Pour batter into two greased loaf pans.

Bake for about 45 minutes if using sm. pans or about 1 hour if using larger pans.

Cool before slicing.

Bread is moist and freezes well and will keep for some time.

Note: Brown sugar may be used instead of white.

Beer Bread

We received this recipe many years ago from our friend, Diane Deeran.

INGREDIENTS:

3 c. self-rising flour
3 T. sugar
1 12-oz. can of beer

DIRECTIONS:

Preheat oven to 150 degrees.

Mix all ingredients and bake at 150 degrees for 10–15 minutes.

Turn oven temperature up to 350 degrees and continue to bake for 40–45 minutes.

cookies, bars and candy

Mom has been in a cookie exchange with her bridge club for over forty years. For a while, she was also in a neighborhood exchange. She would make dozens of rosettes each year. In 1999, Annie, Melissa and I started a cookie exchange. Instead of serving coffee and a festive dessert, we call our exchange "Cookies & Cocktails" (aka "Not Your Mama's Cookie Exchange"). These next few recipes come from our exchange. You'll find Mom's rosette recipe in the Norwegian Treats section.

Chocolate Surprise Cookies

Annie's son Sam loves these and wonders why they can't just keep the whole batch!

INGREDIENTS:

1 bag Hershey®'s Kisses (chocolate) or Dove® chocolates

1 c. butter, softened

⅓ c. sugar

⅓ c. brown sugar

1 t. vanilla extract

2 c. all purpose flour

DIRECTIONS:

Preheat oven to 375 degrees.

Remove wrappers from candy.

Beat butter, sugar and vanilla together in a lg. bowl until well blended.

Add flour to butter mixture; blend until smooth.

Mold about one tablespoon of dough into a ball and wrap around chocolate.

Place on parchment-lined cookie sheet.

Bake 10–12 minutes or until set. Cool slightly.

Drizzle with chocolate drizzle (recipe follows).

Drizzle

¼ cup chocolate chips

1 t. vegetable shortening

Place both ingredients in microwavable bowl. Heat at high setting for 30 seconds; stir.

If necessary, microwave again for 20 seconds until chocolate is melted and smooth.

Ellie's Dog, Lilly, get's a little too close to the action.

Auntie Boo's Chocolate Mint Cookies

These are just like Thin Mint Girl Scout Cookies®. As my Mom would say, they add a little color to a cookie plate.

INGREDIENTS:

¾ c. butter

1-½ c. dark brown sugar, packed

2 T. water

12 oz. chocolate chips

2 eggs

2-½ c. flour

1-¼ t. baking soda

½ t. salt

green chocolate mint Andes® candies

DIRECTIONS:

Preheat oven to 300 degrees.

In a heavy saucepan on low heat, heat butter, sugar and water until butter is melted. Add chocolate chips and stir until partly melted. Remove from stove and stir until all are melted.

Pour into mixing bowl and let cool 10 minutes. Beat in eggs one at a time.

Beat in dry ingredients until blended. Chill one hour.

Line cookie sheets with parchment paper. Roll 1 t. dough into a ball. Continue into all dough is used.

Place balls 2 in. apart on the prepared cookie sheet.

Bake for 10–13 minutes. Remove from oven and immediately press a mint onto each hot cookie. Let cookies cool a few minutes on the baking sheet.

After mint melts, drag a mini-whisk through each mint to make a marble design.

Place cookies on wire racks to cool completely.

notes

Melissa's Natches

These are the best. Melissa got this recipe from her sister, Mandy Ewest.

INGREDIENTS:

15 whole graham crackers
2 sticks unsalted butter
1 c. dark brown sugar, packed
1 t. vanilla extract
1-⅓ c. toasted pecans, chopped
1 6-oz. package semisweet chocolate chips

DIRECTIONS:

Preheat oven to 350 degrees.
Lightly butter 11x17-in. cookie sheet.
Put graham crackers side by side, with edges touching, on the cookie sheet.
Stir butter and brown sugar in pan over med. heat until the butter melts and the sugar dissolves.
Stir in vanilla and boil 1 minute.
Pour caramel over crackers.
Sprinkle with chopped toasted pecans.
Bake 10 minutes until cookies are bubbling and brown.
Remove from oven and sprinkle chocolate chips over cookies.
Cool 4 minutes; cut along edges to separate.
Take cookies off the pan to cool completely; cut each in half.

notes

Annie's Cut-Out Cookies

Nobody makes better cut-out cookies than Annie. I think the reason I love them so much is her frosting.

INGREDIENTS:

1-½ c. powdered sugar
1 c. butter, softened
1 egg
1 t. vanilla
½ t. almond extract
2-½ c. flour
1 t. baking soda
1 t. cream of tartar
½ t. nutmeg

DIRECTIONS:

Mix powdered sugar, butter, egg, vanilla and almond extract.

Sift together flour, baking soda, nutmeg and cream of tartar. Add to wet mixture. Cover and refrigerate at least 2 hours.

Heat oven to 375 degrees.

Divide dough and roll onto floured surface. Cut into shapes.

Transfer to parchment-lined baking sheets. Bake until edges are light brown, 7–8 minutes.

Cookies may be sprinkled with decorator sugar before baking or frosted when cooled.

Frosting:

Annie says she really doesn't have a recipe for her frosting...she just mixes enough powdered sugar, water and almond extract to get the texture and taste she likes. I'd start with the following and adjust as you see fit.

4 c. powdered sugar
3-4 T. milk
2 t. vanilla extract

Mix ingredients together.

If you want to create different colors, place frosting in different bowls and add a few drops of food coloring to each bowl.

Almond Roca Cookies

INGREDIENTS:

2-½ c. all purpose flour
½ t. baking soda
¼ t. salt
1 c. dark brown sugar
½ c. sugar
1 c. butter, room temperature
2 eggs, room temperature
2 t. pure vanilla extract
1 pkg. toffee bits
1 c. coarsely ground almonds
4 oz. milk chocolate
½ T. vegetable oil

DIRECTIONS:

Preheat oven to 300 degrees.

In a med. mixing bowl, whisk together flour, baking soda and salt. Set aside.

In the bowl of an electric mixer, blend sugars together on med. speed. Add butter and mix to form a grainy paste.

Add eggs and vanilla to mixer bowl and mix at med. speed until light and fluffy. Reduce speed to low.

Slowly add the flour mixture to the mixer bowl, then add the toffee bits. Mix until just blended; do not over-mix.

Place almonds in a sm. bowl. Using hands, roll balls of dough into 1- to 1-½-in. balls, then roll in ground nuts.

Place balls on cookie sheets several inches apart. Bake approximately 22 minutes and then transfer cookies to a cooling rack.

Melt the chocolate with the vegetable oil in a double boiler or a bowl set over a pan of simmering water.

Drizzle melted chocolate over cookies.

Place cookies on a cookie sheet and place in freezer or refrigerator until chocolate is firmly set.

Grandma Gina's Chocolate Chip Cookies

For many reasons, Mom and Dad make a perfect couple. Mom likes crusts and crunchy edges and Dad prefers the moist middles of most foods. I think this is why he loves these cookies. Grandma Gina's secret ingredient makes these cookies soft and moist.

INGREDIENTS:

2-¼ c. flour
1 t. soda
1 c. butter
¾ c. brown sugar
¼ c. white sugar
1 t. vanilla extract
1 pkg. instant vanilla pudding mix (3 ¾-oz. pkg.) (This is the SECRET INGREDIENT!)
2 eggs
1 12-oz. pkg. chocolate chips

DIRECTIONS:

Preheat oven to 375 degrees.
Sift first two ingredients together and set aside.
Combine next five ingredients. Beat until creamy and smooth.
Beat in eggs.
Gradually add the flour mixture. Stir in chocolate chips.
Bake on a greased cookie sheet for 8–10 minutes or until lightly browned.

Double Peanut Butter Cookies

This is another recipe from Alice Hermer.

INGREDIENTS:

1 c. butter, softened
1-½ c. sugar
⅔ c. peanut butter
2 eggs
1 t. vanilla extract
2-½ c. flour
1 t. baking soda
½ t. salt
2 c. peanut butter chips

DIRECTIONS:

Preheat oven to 350 degrees.
Beat butter, sugar and peanut butter until creamy.
Add egg and vanilla; beat well.
Blend in flour, baking soda and salt. Stir in chips.
Drop spoonfuls of batter onto parchment-lined baking sheet.
Bake 10–14 minutes.
Makes 6 dozen.

Lemon Bars

At large gatherings, there is sure to be a display of bars. Mom will bake for days leading up to the event and freeze her bars so she can have a wide variety for her guests. They look great displayed on one of those three-tiered plate holders. The key to a good tray of bars is having a wide variety! Here are recipes for some of our favorites.

INGREDIENTS:

Crust

- 1 c. butter or margarine, softened
- 2 c. flour
- ½ c. powdered sugar

DIRECTIONS:

Preheat oven to 350 degrees.

Mix all ingredients together and pat into 9x13-in. pan.

Bake 10–15 minutes.

Filling

- 2 c. sugar
- 4 T. flour
- 1 t. baking powder
- 4 eggs, beaten
- 4 T. lemon juice

Sift together sugar and flour.

In a separate bowl, combine eggs and lemon juice.

Add dry ingredients to wet ingredients; stir to combine.

Pour onto baked crust and bake for 25 minutes. Top bars with frosting (recipe follows).

Frosting

- 3 c. powdered sugar
- 2–4 T. lemon juice

Whisk together sugar and enough lemon juice to reach desired consistency.

Sam, Patrick, and Jack enjoy goodies at the lake

Platinum Blondies

Annie makes these for many family gatherings. They are an excellent update to a classic recipe. Sometimes she mixes white chocolate chips and milk chocolate chips.

INGREDIENTS:

1 ¾ c. brown sugar, packed
2 lg. eggs
1 T. plus 1 t. vanilla extract
1 c. unsalted butter, melted
3 c. all-purpose flour
1 t. baking soda
¼ t. salt
2 c. chopped pecans, toasted
6 oz. white chocolate, chopped or in chip form

DIRECTIONS:

Preheat oven to 325 degrees.

Butter a cake pan.

Beat sugar and egg until light and fluffy, about 3 minutes. Add the vanilla and butter; beat to mix well.

In a sm. bowl, stir together the flour, baking soda and salt. Add dry ingredients to the butter mixture, beating until just incorporated. Do not over-mix.

Using a spoon, stir in the pecans and white chocolate.

Spoon the batter into the prepared pan and use a flat metal spatula or a butter knife to smooth the top. Bake the blondies for 25–30 minutes, until the top is dry and golden and knife inserted in the center comes out with just a few crumbs attached (not wet, but not perfectly dry).

Remove the pan from the oven and place on a wire rack to cool. Cut the blondies into 2-in. squares.

The blondies can be stored, well wrapped, at room temperature for up to 3 days or frozen for up to 2 months.

Special "K" Bars

This is a family favorite. Mom makes them for all of our gatherings and often sends them with Dad on fishing and hunting trips. Because we love them so much, this recipe has been revised to fit in a lg. baking sheet (16 ½x12 in.).

INGREDIENTS:

1 c. white sugar

1 c. white corn syrup

1-½ c. peanut butter

7 c. Rice Krispies®

DIRECTIONS:

Heat sugar and syrup in microwave until sugar dissolves. Add peanut butter.

Spray a bowl and spoon with vegetable spray. Add Rice Krispies® to bowl.

Pour syrup mixture over cereal and stir with greased spoon.

Butter cookie sheet and spread mixture onto the sheet. Press cereal mixture down into pan.

Frosting:

12 oz. chocolate chips

12 oz. butterscotch chips

Melt together and frost.

Brownies

INGREDIENTS:

¼ lb. butter or margarine

1 c. sugar

4 eggs

1 T. vanilla extract

¼ t. salt

1 c. plus 1 T. flour

1 lb. can Hershey®'s Syrup, chocolate

1 c. nuts

DIRECTIONS:

Preheat oven to 350 degrees.

Mix together all ingredients and put in greased and floured 10 ½ x13-in. jelly roll pan. Bake for 30 minutes.

Let cookies cool, then frost (frosting recipe follows).

Frosting:

6 T. butter or margarine

6 T. milk

1-½ c. sugar

pinch of salt

½ c. chocolate chips

Combine butter, milk, sugar and salt in a saucepan and bring to a boil.

Boil for 30 seconds, take off heat and add chips. Beat until right consistency.

Mounds Bars

INGREDIENTS:

½ c. butter or margarine, softened

1-¼ c. sugar

3 T. cocoa (heaping)

1 c. flour

3 eggs

1 c. nuts

2 c. flaked coconut

1 can Eagle Brand® Sweetened condensed milk

DIRECTIONS:

Preheat oven to 325 degrees.

Mix first six ingredients together and spread batter into a 9x13-in. pan

Bake for 15 minutes. Remove from oven.

Combine coconut and condensed milk in a bowl; pour over bars.

Bake again for 20 minutes.

While the bars are baking, mix frosting (recipe follows) and spread when bars are done but still hot.

Frosting:

2 squares semi-sweet chocolate

2 T. butter

powdered sugar

milk as needed

Peanut Butter Cups

If you like Reese's® candies, you are going to love these no-bake bars from Mom.

INGREDIENTS:

1 lb. powdered sugar

½ lb. butter (very soft)

1 c. peanut butter

⅓ lb. crushed graham crackers (1 pkg.)

DIRECTIONS:

Combine all ingredients; press into 9x13-in. pan.

Frost (frosting recipe follows).

Frosting:

2 c. chocolate chips, melted

OR

1 c. chocolate chips, melted
1 c. butterscotch chips, melted

Melissa's Shortbread

You just can't go wrong with this recipe!

INGREDIENTS:

2 c. butter, softened

½ c. brown sugar, firmly packed

½ c. granulated white sugar

2 t. vanilla extract

⅔ c. white rice flour

3 ⅓ c. flour

Butter a 9x13-in. pan.

DIRECTIONS:

Preheat oven to 325 degrees.

In lg. bowl, beat butter, sugars and vanilla together until light and fluffy.

Combine rice flour and regular flour; stir into butter mixture just until smooth and no longer crumbly.

Press dough evenly into buttered pan.

Bake until golden brown and somewhat springy to the touch (45–50 minutes). Cool in pan on wire rack until slightly warm.

Cut into bars. Remove from pan when completely cool.

Note: These bars may be frozen.

Orange Brownies

I made these for Mom and Dad's surprise seventieth birthday party. We always manage to surprise them because we celebrate about six months AFTER their birthdays!

INGREDIENTS:

1-½ c. all purpose flour

1-¾ c. sugar

1 t. salt

1 c. (2 sticks) butter, softened

4 eggs

2 t. pure orange extract

1 t. grated orange zest

DIRECTIONS:

Preheat oven to 350 degrees and grease a 9x13x2-in. pan and set aside.

In a mixing bowl, stir together flour, sugar and salt.

Add butter, eggs, orange extract and orange zest and beat with a handheld electric mixer until well blended.

Pour batter into prepared pan and bake for 30 minutes, or until light golden brown and set.

Remove from oven and pierce top of entire cake with a fork. Drizzle glaze over cake (recipe follows). Cool cake and cut into squares.

Glaze:

¾ c. powdered sugar

2 T. orange juice

1 t. grated orange zest

Combine all ingredients in a bowl, stirring until smooth.

Grandma Gina's Mocha Cakes

Grandma Gina made some AMAZING treats, but these had to be the BEST. These are the most laborious creations, and she always had a batch of them in her freezer. When Joel, Annie and I stopped by on our way out of town to return to college or our apartments in the cities, she would load us up with goodies. When we'd get back to the cities, our roommates were much more excited to see the goody trays than us!

INGREDIENTS:

4 eggs, separated
2 c. sugar
1 c. hot water
2 c. flour
2 t. baking powder
2 t. vanilla extract
½ t. salt

DIRECTIONS:

Preheat oven to 350 degrees and grease and flour bottom only of 10x14-in. pan.

In a separate bowl, beat egg whites until stiff. Set aside.

In another bowl, sift flour, baking powder and salt; set aside.

Cream together egg yolks and sugar. Add dry ingredients alternatively with hot water. Beat well; add vanilla. Fold in egg whites.

Pour batter into pan and bake for 50 minutes or until done. Cool.

Cut into squares and frost with very thin powdered sugar frosting (recipe follows below). Dip top of bars into ground peanuts.

Powdered Sugar Frosting:

4 c. powdered sugar
½ c. butter
3-4 T. milk
2 t. vanilla extract

Mix ingredients together.

Peanut Clusters

Mom got this recipe from our friend Carol Boruff.

INGREDIENTS:

24 oz. white almond bark
12 oz. semi-sweet chocolate chips
12 oz. milk chocolate chips
2 lbs. Spanish peanuts

DIRECTIONS:

Melt bark and chocolate in microwave on defrost for 5 minutes; stir. Continue heating and stirring until fully melted.

Add peanuts to melted mixture.

Drop by spoonfuls onto waxed paper. Cool.

Chocolate-Covered Cherries

When I was in high school, I dated a guy who loved chocolate covered cherries. Mom found this recipe and I made him homemade chocolate covered cherries for Christmas and Valentine's Day. They are really good, but a bit putsy and time-consuming.

INGREDIENTS:

Filling:
4 c. powdered sugar
½ lb. butter
2 T. milk
1 t. vanilla extract

Mix all ingredients together and refrigerate over night.

Cherry Middles:
1-½ jars cherries

DIRECTIONS:

Cover hands in powdered sugar to prevent mixture from sticking to hands. Roll powdered sugar into balls, flatten balls and wrap mixture around cherries.

Put on waxed paper on cookie sheet. Freeze overnight.

Chocolate Covering:
6 squares semi-sweet chocolate
4 squares unsweetened chocolate
¼ square paraffin wax

Melt the chocolate and wax together in a double boiler.

Take only 20 cherries out of freezer at a time. Use toothpick to dip in melted chocolate. Refrigerate.

Note: These can be stored in the freezer.

desserts, cakes and pies

Danish Christmas Day Pudding

Each year, Mom makes this delicious almond rice pudding on Christmas Day. In one of the servings, she hides a whole almond. The person who is served the pudding with the almond wins the prize. The winner is responsible for buying the prize the following year. In our minds, it is a Norwegian tradition!

INGREDIENTS:

¼ c. rice, uncooked

2 c. milk

¼ c. almonds, chopped very fine

1 ¼-oz. envelope unflavored gelatin, dissolved in ¼ c. water

2 c. cream, whipped

1 t. vanilla extract

5 T. sugar

1 whole almond

DIRECTIONS:

Cook rice and milk together until rice is tender.

Add chopped almonds and dissolved gelatin to cooked rice.

When cool, add cream, vanilla, sugar and the whole almond.

Spoon pudding into individual serving dishes. (Actually, I think Mom strategically buries the almond in one of the servings. I've seen her intentionally rig it so she and Dad do not win.)

This recipe makes 7 generous servings.

Peppermint Dessert

Each year Joel requests this dessert for our Christmas Eve gathering. It is a very easy and festive dessert.

INGREDIENTS:

Crust

- 2 c. graham cracker crumbs
- ½ c. butter, softened

Combine and pat into a 9 x 13-in. pan and chill.

Filling

- 3 eggs
- 3 squares chocolate, melted
- ½ c. butter, softened
- 1-½ c. powdered sugar

Mix and beat well and put on top of crust. Chill again until firm.

Topping

- 1-½ pt. cream, whipped
- 1 10 oz. pkg marshmallows
- pink or green food coloring
- ½ c. peppermint candy canes, crushed

DIRECTIONS:

Mix together whipped cream, marshmallows and crushed candy canes. Spread over chilled desert. Sprinkle with one crushed candy cane.

Chill overnight.

notes

Cajun Bread Pudding with Rum Sauce

This is another recipe Annie and Paul picked up in New Orleans. She serves this at their annual "Fat Tuesday" fête. It's best with loads of vanilla ice cream or whipped cream…or both!

INGREDIENTS:

¾ loaf stale French bread

3 c. milk or melted vanilla ice cream

4 eggs

1 c. sugar

1-½ t. vanilla

1 t. cinnamon

½ t. salt

¾ c. raisins

DIRECTIONS:

Preheat oven to 350 degrees and butter a 2-qt. baking dish.

Break the bread into med. pieces and moisten with 1 c. of milk. Let stand.

Beat eggs. Add sugar, vanilla, cinnamon, salt, 2 c. of milk and raisins into eggs.

Pour mixture over soaked bread and stir gently. Pour into buttered baking dish. Bake for 45 minutes to 1 hour or until a toothpick inserted in center comes out clean.

To serve, top with rum sauce (recipe follows).

Makes 8 to 10 servings.

Rum Sauce

4 t. cornstarch

⅓ c. water

2 T. butter

¾ c. fruit juice or water (any fruit juice will work)

¼ c. brown sugar

¼ c. white rum

Mix cornstarch in water in a saucepan. Place on med. heat and stir until mixture thickens.

Add butter and stir until melted.

Add fruit juice and brown sugar; stir well. Add white rum and stir until blended.

Simmer on low heat for 10 minutes, stirring occasionally.

Spoon hot over bread pudding.

Filled Strawberries

These fresh fruit desserts are like bites of strawberry cheesecake. They look impressive, but are very easy to make. Annie started serving them at Sam and Ellie's baptisms and First Communion parties. They're not just for religious celebrations…she's served them at her "Martinis for Moms" parties, too.

INGREDIENTS:

6 oz. cream cheese, at room temperature
½ t. pure vanilla
1-½ T. powdered sugar
12 lg. strawberries

DIRECTIONS:

Beat cream cheese, powdered sugar and vanilla until fluffy.

Trim bottom of strawberries so each stands upright. Use a melon baller to scoop out stems and tops.

Fill a pastry bag fitted with a ½-in. star top with the cream cheese mixture.

Pipe cream cheese mixture into strawberries until cream cheese brims over the tops.

Berries can be topped with sliced and toasted almonds.

notes

Berries in the Snow

During my junior year, Mom and Dad hosted a dinner for two couples before the annual Jobs Daughter Formal Dance at the Kato Ballroom. My sister Annie wore a black skirt and white shirt and she served as our waitress. This was the very fancy dessert Mom made for us.

INGREDIENTS:

6 egg whites
½ t. cream of tartar
1 t. salt
1-¾ c. granulated sugar
1 8-oz. pkg. cream cheese, softened
1 c. granulated sugar
1 t. vanilla extract
1 pt. whipping cream, whipped
2 c. miniature marshmallows
1 pt. strawberries, sliced

DIRECTIONS:

Preheat oven to 275 degrees.

Beat egg whites, cream of tartar and salt until frothy. Gradually add 1-¾ c. sugar, beating until stiff, about 10–15 minutes.

Spread mixture into a greased 9x13-in. pan. Bake for 60 minutes. Cool.

In a separate bowl, beat cream cheese, 1 c. sugar and vanilla. Fold in whipped cream and then marshmallows.

Spread evenly over cooled egg white mixture.

Refrigerate overnight.

Top with strawberries just before serving.

For fancy occasions, Mom would make individual servings of snow. (Mom made me replace the word "piles" with servings.) She'd make 4–5-in. circles of meringue on parchment paper instead of spreading it in the pan.

Sweet Cream Ice Cream

When we were growing up, it was a real treat to get homemade ice cream. The anticipation after packing the tub with ice and rock salt and cranking it for what seemed like forever was almost unbearable…and when they'd take off the cover and remove the beater…oh, there is no better taste. Mom always talks about being a little girl and waiting around for the ice cream and realizing that the batch had been spoiled when some rock salt got into the tub…what a disappointment. Thankfully, ice cream makers have vastly improved. I LOVE ice cream and this is my all-time favorite recipe.

INGREDIENTS:

2 lg. eggs
¾ c. sugar
2 c. heavy or whipping cream
1 c. milk

DIRECTIONS:

Whisk the eggs in a mixing bowl until light and fluffy, 1–2 minutes.

Whisk in the sugar, a little at a time, then continue whisking until completely blended, about 1 minute more.

Pour in the cream and milk and whisk to blend.

Follow your ice cream maker's instructions to freeze.

Makes 1 quart.

Mandarin Orange Dessert

This is another light and easy recipe from Mom. She loves it because she can keep all the ingredients in her pantry.

INGREDIENTS:

1 pkg. yellow cake mix (plain)

3 eggs

¾ c. oil

1 sm can of mandarin oranges, with juice

DIRECTIONS:

Preheat oven to 375 degrees.

Beat together all the ingredients, (Including oranges)

Pour batter into a greased 9x13-in. pan. Bake for 30 minutes.

Cool completely, then frost (frosting recipe follows).

Frosting

1 8-oz. tub Cool Whip® whipped topping

1 t. vanilla extract

1 sm. box instant pudding, vanilla

20 oz. crushed pineapple with juice

Directions:

Mix together all ingredients. Spread on cake and refrigerate.

Kahlua® Cream Dessert

I made these for a post-holiday gathering in 2004 with my college roommates and their husbands. Vanessa and Dave Hoek and Jenn and Alvaro Fernandez gave this rave reviews. It couldn't be any easier and it is very light…not even enough Kahlua to give Jenn bed-spins!

INGREDIENTS:

2 c. Cool Whip® whipped topping

1 pt. softened vanilla ice cream

¼ c. Kahlua®

toasted slivered almonds

DIRECTIONS:

Beat whipping cream until stiff.

Blend in ice cream and Kahlua®.

Pour into wine glasses.

Freeze until firm.

To serve, garnish with toasted slivered almonds.

Serves 4.

Cherry Cheese Trifle

There is a family joke...if folks see me bring in a trifle, I've screwed something up. Trifles are a great way to hide mistakes. This trifle is AWESOME! Contrary to popular belief, there've been a few trifles I've actually planned to make! :)

INGREDIENTS:

1 8-oz. pkg. cream cheese, softened
1 14-oz. can sweetened condensed milk
1 12-oz. container frozen whipped topping, thawed and divided
½ t. almond extract
1 13-oz. prepared angel food cake
2 21-oz. cans cherry pie filling

In a med. bowl, combine cream cheese and sweetened condensed milk. Beat with an electric mixer until smooth. Stir in ½ of whipped topping and almond extract; set aside.

DIRECTIONS:

Tear angel food cake into 1-in. pieces.

Place ⅓ of cake pieces in bottom of a trifle bowl. Spoon ⅓ of cream cheese filling over cake and top with ⅓ of pie filling. Repeat layers twice more.

Spread remaining whipped topping over top of trifle, sealing to edges. Garnish with additional pie filling and sliced almonds, if desired.

Strawberry-Kiwi Trifle

This is a wonderful summer dessert from Mom. It's very light and looks very pretty.

INGREDIENTS:

1 angel food cake
1 3-oz. pkg. vanilla instant pudding
2 c. milk
1 8-oz. container Cool Whip® whipped topping
1-½ pt. strawberries, sliced
2 kiwis, peeled and sliced

DIRECTIONS:

Trim brown crust from cake and tear into 1-in. pieces.

Prepare pudding according to package instructions and fold in the Cool Whip®.

Place ½ of cake pieces in trifle bowl. Add ½ pudding mix, ½ berries and ½ of kiwi slices. Repeat layers.

Refrigerate overnight (or at least for 4 hours).

Lemon Curd Trifle with Fresh Berries

We usually celebrate Annie's birthday on Mother's Day. And after the BBQ rib feast Dad creates, we need a light dessert. In 2006, I served this trifle in place of a birthday cake.

INGREDIENTS:

6 lg. egg yolks
1 c. sugar
4 lemons, zested and juiced
1 stick unsalted butter, cut in chunks
1 pt. fresh strawberries, stemmed and sliced in half lengthwise
1 pt. fresh blueberries
1 pt. fresh raspberries
2 c. Cool Whip® whipped topping
1 prepared lemon pound cake, sliced
¼ c. Grand Marnier (optional)

DIRECTIONS:

To make the lemon curd, bring a pot of water to a simmer over med.-low heat.

Combine the egg yolks, sugar, lemon juice and zest in a metal or glass heat-resistant bowl and whisk until smooth.

Set the bowl over the simmering water, without letting the bottom touch the water and continue to whisk.

Keep working that arm and whisk mixture vigorously for a good 10 minutes, until the curd has doubled in volume and is very thick and yellow. Don't let it boil!

Remove the bowl from heat and whisk in the butter, a couple of chunks at a time, until melted.

Refrigerate until the custard is cold and firm.

To build the trifle, put the berries in a mixing bowl and toss them together so they are evenly distributed.

Fold the whipped topping into the chilled lemon curd to lighten it up into a mousse.

Line a glass trifle bowl with pieces of pound cake to fit. Drizzle or brush the cake with the Grand Marnier®.

Spoon a layer of the lemon curd over the cake and then a layer of mixed berries. Repeat the layers until the ingredients are used up; the last layer looks best if it's the berries.

Chill before serving.

Chocolate Trifle

In 2006, my friend, Betsy Fjelland, wanted a low-key birthday celebration at her apartment. I volunteered to bring dessert. All she wanted was something chocolate. This certainly worked!

INGREDIENTS:

1 19.8-oz. pkg. brownie mix and all ingredients listed on brownie packaging

1 3.9-oz. pkg. instant chocolate pudding mix

½ c. water

1 14-oz. can sweetened condensed milk

1 8-oz. container Cool Whip® whipped topping (thawed)

1 12-oz. container Cool Whip® ehipped topping (thawed)

1 1-½ oz. bar chocolate

DIRECTIONS:

Prepare and bake brownies according to package directions and cool completely.

Cut brownies into 1-in. squares.

In a lg. bowl, combine pudding mix, water and sweetened condensed milk. Mix until smooth.

Fold in 8 oz. Cool Whip® until no streaks remain.

In a trifle bowl or glass serving dish, layer half of the brownies, half of the pudding mixture and half of the 12 oz. Cool Whip. Repeat layers.

Shave chocolate onto top layer for garnish.

Refrigerate at least 8 hours before serving.

Pistachio Bundt Cake

Growing up, this was one of my favorite cakes. This recipe came from a local Mankato grocery store, Madsen's. Our Grandma Gina worked at Madsen's for a number of years. I always thought this cake looked so cool when it was cut.

INGREDIENTS:

1 pkg. white cake mix

1 pkg. instant pistachio pudding (3.5 oz.)

½ c. oil

1 c. water or orange juice

4 eggs

1 t. vanilla extract

¾ c. chocolate syrup

DIRECTIONS:

Preheat oven to 350 degrees.

Combine cake mix and instant pudding in lg. bowl with oil, water, eggs and vanilla extract. Blend well.

Pour ⅔ of batter into a well-greased and floured Bundt pan.

To remaining batter add chocolate syrup, mixing well.

Pour chocolate batter on top of batter in pan. Do not stir.

Bake for 55 minutes or until cake tests done. Cool 10 minutes before removing from pan.

Aloha Cake

When Annie was in high school, she played on the Mankato East golf team. Her coach didn't know how serious her golf game was, but he knew she was serious about her tan. Annie's birthday is April 16th so Mom decided to surprise her with a cake after golf practice. She took this cake out to the Terrace View Club House and when Annie walked in, the surprised birthday girl said, "Mom, what are you doing here?"

INGREDIENTS:

1 pkg. yellow cake mix and all ingredients listed on packaging

11 oz. cream cheese (room temp)

1 sm. pkg. instant vanilla pudding

1 c. milk

1 21-oz. can crushed pineapple

1 12-oz. container Cool Whip® whipped topping

Toppings:

crushed nuts; dry, shredded coconut; halved maraschino cherries.

DIRECTIONS:

Prepare yellow cake according to package instructions. Pour batter into a jellyroll pan and bake according to cake directions. Cool cake.

Beat cream cheese to soften. Add pudding and milk and cream mixture well.

Spread mixture on cooled cake.

Drain pineapple. Spread on top of cream cheese.

Spread Cool Whip® over pineapple.

Sprinkle with finely chopped nuts, coconut and halved maraschino cherries. Refrigerate.

Serves 12 - 15.

Snicker Cake

Joel and I were born on the same day, seven years apart. Growing up, Mom always made two cakes for us. Joel's favorite cake is German chocolate. If you know anything about German chocolate cakes, they are a lot of work. I think there were a few years she got away using this cake instead.

INGREDIENTS:

1 box German chocolate cake mix and all ingredients listed on packaging

⅔ c. evaporated milk

¾ c. margarine, softened

1 c. chocolate chips

1 14-oz. pkg. caramels

1 c. chopped nuts

DIRECTIONS:

Preheat oven to 350 degrees.

Mix cake ingredients according to instructions on package.

Add ⅓ c. evaporated milk, nuts and margarine to the batter. Fold to incorporate.

Pour half of the batter into greased and floured 9x13-in. pan.

Bake for 20 minutes and cool completely.

While cake is baking, melt caramels and ⅓ c. evaporated milk together.

Pour caramel mixture over baked cake.

Sprinkle with chocolate chips. Not w/Carmels

Pour remaining uncooked cake batter over caramel layer.

Bake at 350 degrees for 25–30 minutes.

Raw Apple Cake

This is awesome and VERY easy! I don't always eat my apples while they are crispy… this is my favorite way to use them up.

INGREDIENTS:

2 c. sugar
1 stick butter
2 eggs
1 t. vanilla extract
2 c. flour
2 t. baking soda
1 t. salt
1 t. cinnamon
4 c. chopped, unpeeled apples

DIRECTIONS:

Preheat oven to 350 degrees and grease a 9x13-in. pan.

Cream sugar and butter together. Add eggs and vanilla; beat well.

Add dry ingredients and apples. Mix well.

Pour into prepared pan.

Bake 35–40 minutes.

Top hot cake with glaze (recipe follows).

Serves 12-15.

Note: If you choose to omit the glaze, you may dust with powdered sugar. And this cake is great with whipped cream or ice cream!

Glaze

1 c. powdered sugar
2 T. butter
2 T. milk or cream
½ t. vanilla extract

Combine all ingredients together until smooth.

Rhubarb Upside-Down Cake

When I moved to Minneapolis, I discovered that I was a proud owner of a great rhubarb plant. During the early summer, I'm always trying new rhubarb recipes. This is one of my very easy favorites. It is nice and gooey—Just the way Dad and I like it!

INGREDIENTS:

1 yellow cake mix and all ingredients listed on packaging
1 c. sugar
3 c. rhubarb or apples
2 c. half-and-half

DIRECTIONS:

Preheat oven to 350 degrees.
Mix yellow cake mix according to package directions.
Pour into a 9x13-in. cake pan.
Chop rhubarb and place on top of cake batter.
Sprinkle sugar over rhubarb.
Pour 2 cups half-and-half on top.
Bake for 45 minutes.
Cool before serving.

notes

Honey-Lemon Rhubarb Pie

Dad LOVES this pie. He just wishes Mom would make it more often!

INGREDIENTS:

4 c. rhubarb, cut into ½-in. pieces
1-½ c. sugar
6 T. flour
¼ t. salt
2 t. lemon rind, grated
⅓ c. strained honey
4-5 drops red food coloring
pastry for 2 9-in. crusts
2 T. butter

DIRECTIONS:

Preheat oven to 450 degrees.

Combine rhubarb, sugar, flour, salt and lemon rind; mix well. Blend in honey and food coloring. Let stand while making pastry.

Line a 9-in. pie plate with one pastry crust. Fill with rhubarb mixture; dot with butter. Adjust top crust over filling and seal edges. (For a sparkling top, brush with milk and sprinkle with sugar.)

Bake 10 minutes; reduce heat to 350 degrees and bake 35–45 minutes more.

notes

Sour Cherry Pie

This is Annie's classic cherry pie. She makes it extra sour, because that is the way Paul likes it. I love the almond flavor.

INGREDIENTS:

⅔ c. sugar

⅓ c. flour

3 16-oz. cans pitted red tart cherries, drained

½ t. almond extract

pastry, for two 9-in. round crusts (I use Pappy's® Pie Crust Dough, which is frozen, or boxed pie crust mix)

DIRECTIONS:

Heat oven to 425 degrees.

Prepare pastry.

Mix sugar and flour; stir in cherries. Turn filling into pastry-lined 9-in. pie plate; sprinkle with almond extract.

Cover with top crust. Make slits in top crust. Seal and flute. Cover edge with 2–3-in. strip of aluminum foil to prevent excessive browning; remove foil during last 15 minutes of baking.

Bake until crust is brown and juice begins to bubble though slits in crust, 35–45 minutes.

notes

Whoopie Pies

Annie and Sam were first introduced to Whoopie Pies while watching *Unwrapped* on the Food Network. They searched the Internet for a recipe and this is a variation on what they found. The kids love these!

INGREDIENTS:

3 c. sugar
1 c. butter
4 eggs
½ c. vegetable oil
1 T. vanilla extract
6 c. all purpose flour
2 c. unsweetened cocoa power
1 t. baking powder
1-½ t. baking soda
1 t. salt
3 c. milk

DIRECTIONS:

Preheat oven to 350 degrees.

In a lg. bowl, beat the sugar, butter and eggs together until well combined. Add the oil and vanilla extract and beat again.

In a separate bowl, combine all of the dry ingredients. Add half of the dry mixture to the egg mixture and beat or stir to blend. Add 1-½ cups milk and beat again. Add the remaining dry mixture and beat until incorporated. Add the remaining milk and beat until well blended.

With a lg. spoon, spoon out 32 circles of batter onto parchment-lined baking sheets.

Bake 10–12 minutes and let cool.

Spread filling (recipe follows) onto 16 circles and top with remaining 16 circles.

FILLING

2 sticks unsalted butter, room temperature
2 c. powdered sugar
1 jar (7 ½-oz.) Marshmallow Fluff®
2 t. vanilla

Cream together butter and sugar until pale and fluffy. Add Fluff and vanilla and continue mixing until well combined.

Choc-Marshmallow Pie

This is a favorite recipe from Dad's youth. It is a pie his Grandma Nusser always made for holidays.

INGREDIENTS:

½ lb (32) marshmallows
1 1-oz. square unsweetened chocolate
½ c. milk
1 t. vanilla extract
1 c. heavy cream, whipped
1 9-in. graham cracker crust

DIRECTIONS:

Combine marshmallows, chocolate and milk in top of double boiler. Heat until marshmallows and chocolate are melted. Cool.

Add vanilla and fold in whipped cream.

Pour into graham cracker crust; chill until set.

Serve with a dollop of whipped cream.

Sam's Famous Mud Pie

This was Sam's entry in the kindergarten Thanksgiving pie contest. Sam's mud pie won first place. It is not a surprise that a bunch of five-year-olds will vote on the chocolate pie over the pumpkin or the apple. Sam vividly remembers this event and insists on making the pie every Thanksgiving and any other time Annie will buy the ingredients. You will have leftovers, but that is always okay with the kids.

INGREDIENTS:

1 6-oz. Oreo® Cookie Pie Crust (I used to make my own, but now I just buy the pre-made version)
2 lg. pkgs. chocolate pudding and all ingredients listed on the packaging (I think the heat-and-serve variety of pudding is better than the instant for the pie)
1 box Oreo® Cookie Crumbs, or equivalent amount of Oreo® cookies pulverized in the food processor
1 bag gummy worms

DIRECTIONS:

Make the pudding according to the package directions.

When the pudding is cool but not set, pour it into the crust.

Push a bunch of worms in the pudding. Cover with the Oreo® crumbs.

Add more worms to the pie top. Push some halfway in.

Blushing Apple or Peach Pie

I'm not like Mom and Annie…I avoid my rolling pin at all costs. Sally Brown used this recipe in a 4-H demonstration and it has a "no-roll crust." (I've been making this recipe for years!) It's a no-fail recipe you can whip up in no time! It's great for last-minute company. Over the years, I've made this quite a few times as I tried to impress dates :)

INGREDIENTS:

Pie Filling

1 c. sugar

½ c. flour

¼ t. cinnamon

¼ c. butter, melted

2 c. apple or peach slices, peeled

¼ c. water

No-Roll Crust

1-½ c. flour

2 t. sugar

1 t. salt

½ c. vegetable oil

1 T. milk

1 T. water

DIRECTIONS:

Preheat oven to 425 degrees.

Mix crust ingredients together and press into a pie pan.

Sift dry ingredients together.

Sprinkle ½ of dry ingredients into the pie shell.

Add apple or peach slices. Sprinkle fruit, ¼ c. water and the last of the dry ingredients.

Drizzle with melted butter.

Bake for 15 minutes. Reduce heat to 350 degrees and bake for 30 minutes.

Pumpkin Pie

When Joel was younger, he started a tradition on the night before Thanksgiving. He'd gather all of his buddies at the Stone Toad, now the "Tav on the Ave," for the annual "Turkey Trot." It was a great time to catch up with friends and family when they returned to Kato for the holiday. Mom was usually still up baking when we returned from the "Tav."

We always run out of room in the refrigerator during the holidays and one advantage to living in Minnesota is that your garage doubles as a walk-in fridge. Dad always puts some beer out there, but Mom gets a bit nervous about putting food on the attic steps, as animals may get into it. So she started putting her prepared dishes into the back seat of her car.

One Thanksgiving, Dad walked through his walk-in fridge and came inside and said, "Does anybody know where that case of beer is? It's not in the garage anymore." We all just accused Joel of taking it and blew it off. After our Thanksgiving feast, Mom went to the garage to grab the pies out of the backseat of her car. She came in and said, "What happened to the pie? I made two and there is only one out there." We may not have reacted when Dad's beer was missing, but we were up in arms over a missing pumpkin pie. Mom was really upset because the thief stole the pie that had pecans on top AND it was in her new pie pan! We all still laugh about some guy walking down Agency Road with a case of beer and a pumpkin pie. Mom now locks the door of her walk-in fridge. And hey…she still wants that good pie plate back!

INGREDIENTS:

1 unbaked pastry shell

1 15 oz. can Festival® Golden Pie Pumpkin

3 eggs, slightly beaten

1 c. granulated sugar or light brown sugar

½ t. salt

1 t. cinnamon

¼ t. cloves

¼ t. nutmeg

¼ t. ginger

1-½ c. milk or evaporated milk

DIRECTIONS:

Preheat oven to 400 degrees.

Prepare a one-crust pie shell.

Combine eggs, sugar, salt and spices and beat well. Blend in pumpkin. Add milk and beat well.

Pour pumpkin mixture into pastry-lined pie pan.

Top with pecan topping (recipe follows).

Bake for 10 minutes, then reduce heat and bake at 350 degrees for 40–45 minutes. Pie is done when knife, inserted in center, comes out clean.

Cool before serving.

Pecan Topping

INGREDIENTS:

2 T. brown sugar

1 T. butter, softened

¼ c. pecans, chopped

DIRECTIONS:

Mix all ingredients together and sprinkle over top of pumpkin pie before baking.

notes

norwegian treats

Lefse

One year, Annie decided we should learn about our Norwegian heritage, so she hosted a little Eichers Family Community Education class. Early one Saturday morning, Mom and Gram ventured to Chanhassen with the lefse grill and krumkaka iron. If you are unfamiliar with making lefse, it's a rather delicate process. The dough has to be chilled to the right temperature and the grill needs to be HOT.

Every Christmas, Mom brings the lefse she's purchased at the Bethlehem Lutheran Nordic Bazaar to our celebration. Most of us like to top our lefse with a thin layer of butter and sprinkle it with granulated sugar. The purist Paul Aas just eats it plain. Either way, you really can't go wrong.

This recipe comes from Grandma Gina's friends, Gladys Arneson and Gert DeRemer.

INGREDIENTS:

3 c. mashed or riced potatoes

2 T. butter

2 T. whipping cream

¼ t. salt

1 c. flour

DIRECTIONS:

Make potatoes the day before and cool.

Mix potatoes, butter, whipping cream and salt with pastry blender. Slowly add flour and mix well.

Form mixture into loaves.

Keep loaves in refrigerator, taking out only one at a time. Slice and roll out into a very thin circle and bake on lefse grill at 450 degrees. Use a lefse stick to turn. Place between damp cloths after removing from grill and cool.

Rosettes

When we were growing up, Mom was part of two cookie exchanges: the neighborhood's and her bridge club's. Almost every year she made rosettes. Rosettes are a very delicate, deep-fried cookie. In addition to making these for the cookie exchanges, she'd make many more for gifts and the Bethlehem Lutheran Nordic Bazaar. In 2007, Mom made forty-one dozen rosettes. Mom used popcorn tins to store dozens of these delicate cookies.

INGREDIENTS:

2 eggs, beaten
1 c. water
1 c. milk
3 t. vanilla extract
4 t. sugar
1 t. salt
2 c. Gold Medal Wondra® Specialty Flour

DIRECTIONS:

Combine ingredients.

Fill your largest saucepan, halfway with veg. oil. Heat to 375 degrees. (Use a candy thermometer.)

Heat rosette iron in vegetable oil to 375 degrees. For first rosette, wipe excess oil from iron with paper towel and dip iron into batter, but do not allow batter to come over top of the iron. Put iron back in hot oil. Fry for about 20 seconds, or until desired color.

To remove iron from oil, turn it over to drain. Carefully take rosette off iron and repeat above steps. Mom uses a chopstick to help her remove the rosettes from the iron. Drain rosettes on paper towels.

To serve, dip in granulated or powdered sugar. (Mom uses granulated.)

Makes 5-6 dozen.

Note: Mom stores her rosettes in tins for up to 6 weeks.

Krumkaka

This was another one of Grandma Gina's specialties. The great-grandkids absolutely love these little cones of krumkaka!

INGREDIENTS:

2 eggs
½ c. sugar
⅓ c. corn starch
⅓ c. flour
1 t. vanilla extract
½ c. margarine or butter, melted
margarine for greasing iron

DIRECTIONS:

Beat eggs until light in color.

Gradually beat in sugar until mixture is thick and ivory color.

Gently fold in corn starch, flour and vanilla. Fold in melted butter or margarine.

Heat iron over med. heat; brush lightly with margarine.

Place rounded top of batter on iron.

Close iron; cook until lightly brown. Turn iron; cook until second side is golden brown.

Remove quickly and roll at once on wooden cone to shape. Cool and slip off.

Makes 36.

notes

New Snack Mix

INGREDIENTS:

Crispix® cereal, big box
Bugles®, one box
pretzels, one bag
peanuts, one can/jar
Fritos® brand Corn Chips, one bag
3 sticks of margarine, melted
3 t. garlic salt
3 t. chili powder
3 t. curry powder
3 t. Worcestershire sauce
½ c. brown sugar

DIRECTIONS:

Preheat oven to 250 degrees.

Combine first five ingredients in a lg. paper bag.

Mix remaining ingredients together in a separate bowl.

Divide dry snack mix and place in two lg. roasting pans.

Divide gooey mixture and stir into the dry mix.

Bake for one hour, stirring every 20 minutes.

Oven Roasted Maple Gorp

I made this for a LONG road trip with Joel's family as we headed to our cousin Julie Lilien's wedding in Kansas.

INGREDIENTS:

¾ c. maple syrup
1 cinnamon stick
1 t. vanilla extract
1 c. oats
1 c. peanuts, shelled and peeled
2 c. whole natural almonds
½ c. golden raisins
½ c. Craisins®
½ c. pumpkin seeds, shelled
1 c. M&M's®

DIRECTIONS:

Preheat oven to 375 degrees.

Place maple syrup in a saucepan on the stove with cinnamon and vanilla over med.-low heat to infuse the flavor. Warm syrup for a few minutes; remove.

Combine oats, peanuts, almonds, raisins, Craisins® and pumpkin seeds in a bowl. Toss with maple syrup and remove the cinnamon stick.

Spread the maple-coated mixture on a cookie sheet and roast 15 minutes. Remove the mix from oven and transfer to another cold pan, tossing the mix to quick-cool it. Once cool, toss with M&M's®.

Serves 8.

Mom's Caramel Corn

INGREDIENTS:

5 qt. popped popcorn
2 c. brown sugar
1 c. butter
½ t. salt
½ c. dark corn syrup
½ t. baking soda

DIRECTIONS:

Preheat oven to 250 degrees.

Mix together salt, butter, brown sugar and syrup.

Boil together for 5 minutes; stir in soda.

Pour over popped corn, bake for one hour. Stir every 15 minutes.

Power Bars

Melissa came across this recipe and shared it with me. I packed these for breakfast each morning when I lived with two gals in a one-bathroom duplex. I HAD to work out at the Medtronic fitness center each morning in order to get a shower!

INGREDIENTS:

1-½ c. rolled oats
1 c. crispy brown rice cereal
¼ c. sesame seeds
1-½ c. dried apricots
1-½ c. raisins
½ c. nonfat protein powder
½ c. toasted wheat germ
1 c. light corn syrup
½ c. granulated sugar
½ c. organic peanut butter
1-½ t. vanilla extract
½ t. cinnamon

DIRECTIONS:

Preheat oven to 350.

Spread oats, cereal and sesame seeds in a 13x18-in. nonstick jellyroll pan. Bake, stirring occasionally, until oats are toasted, about 15 minutes.

Meanwhile, chop apricots (I use a food processor), transfer to a lg. bowl.

Add raisins, protein powder and wheat germ; toss with hands to mix.

Stir in hot oat mixture.

Lightly coat jellyroll pan with cooking spray.

In a heavy saucepan over med.-high heat, combine syrup and sugar; bring to boil. Reduce heat to low. Stir in peanut butter, vanilla and cinnamon.

Quickly pour syrup over oatmeal mixture and stir well. With wet hands or wet spatula, immediately spread warm mixture into jellyroll pan, pressing into thin, even layer. If you work too slowly, the mixture will harden and be very difficult to spread.

Cut into 2x3-in. bars.

Makes 30 bars.

Note: Bars can be wrapped individually and stored in an airtight container for up to four weeks in the fridge or frozen for longer storage.

Melissa's Fruit and Nuts Granola

This treat is great with yogurt.

INGREDIENTS:

4 c. rolled oats
2 c. oat bran
1 c. raw sesame seeds
1 c. flax seeds
2 c. raw sunflower seeds
1 c. unsweetened coconut flakes
1 c. almonds, chopped
1 c. walnuts, chopped
1 c. raisins
1 c. dried apricots, diced
1 c. dried papaya
½ c. olive oil
¼ c. honey

DIRECTIONS:

Preheat oven to 325 degrees.

In a lg. roasting pan, mix together oats, bran, seeds, coconut flakes and nuts.

Over a low flame, heat the oil and honey together until the mixture is very thin and easily poured.

Drizzle the oil and honey mixture over the dry ingredients, mixing constantly, until all the pieces are coated evenly.

Bake the granola, stirring thoroughly every 15 minutes or so, until lightly browned, about 45–60 minutes.

When the granola is baked and has cooled slightly, mix the fruit with the granola and stir thoroughly to mix.

After the granola has cooled completely, store in food storage bags in the refrigerator.

miscellaneous

Rhubarb Jam

When Grandma packed up our goodies, she always included a jar of strawberry/ rhubarb jelly. I remember my roommate Vanessa Hoek and I bartering jelly. If she could get an extra jar of her Grandma Brueske's pepper jelly, I'd give her a jar of Grandma Gina's strawberry rhubarb jelly.

INGREDIENTS:

- 5 c. rhubarb, diced
- 3 c. sugar
- 1 3-oz. pkg. strawberry, cherry, or raspberry Jell-O® (Grandma Gina preferred strawberry.)

DIRECTIONS:

Combine rhubarb and sugar. Let stand overnight.

Boil fruit mixture at least 10 minutes.

Remove from heat.

Add Jell-O®.

Stir well and pour into jars.

This has to be refrigerated and can be put in a freezer.

Mama IKES's Pickles

When we kids were growing up on 130 Agency, every August Mom and Dad would make garlic dill pickles. Some years they would can a hundred quarts. Dad would patiently scrub all the cucumbers at the sink. One year, we had lots of rain and the cukes were very dirty and difficult to get clean. Our neighbor Charlene Uble suggested putting them in the washing machine with towels and using the delicate cycle. This would not be approved by the County Extension Office, but it certainly solved our problem!

Mom's pickles were legendary to my classmates. I was fortunate enough to grow up when girls' athletics were starting to take off. Two of my classmates' fathers, Jerry Maschka and Gary Lunz, started a traveling softball team, "The Mankato Peppers." Every weekend, our families would travel out of town and spend loads of hours in the bleachers and in the hotel. To say we "bonded" would be an understatement. Many fan rituals developed, including the opening of Mama IKES's dill pickles at the end of the day. The girls I played ball with back in sixth grade were some of the most talented female athletes in the state. They went on to win state in basketball and softball during high school. Years before, I had moved to the bleachers to cheer them on. But they never forgot Mama IKES's pickles. When they were competing at the tournaments, Mom always managed to get them a couple quarts. I seem to recall Barry Wortel from KTOE even mentioning Mama IKES's famous dill pickles on the radio during one of his post-show wrap-ups.

]INGREDIENTS:

cucumbers (we like the smaller sized cucumbers.)

1 T. sugar per qt. jar

garlic, peeled (a total of approximately 2 heads for 9–10 qt.)

fresh dill

13 c. water

6 c. vinegar

1 c. pickling salt

DIRECTIONS:

Pack cucumbers in jars with sugar and lots of dill (including stems, on bottom and top of jar), 1 T. sugar and 2 cloves of garlic to each qt.

Combine water, vinegar and pickling salt in a lg. pot and bring brine to a boil.

Pour brine over cucumbers and fill jars to top; seal tight. Set jars in boiling water to cover top of jar. Cover with blanket and let stand until cool.

Makes 9–10 qt. per batch.

Note: Four batches uses 9 heads of garlic.

MasterMix "Bisquick"

I started cooking when I was in 4-H. You've heard the expression, it takes a village... When it comes to developing a 4-Her, it takes a family. When I prepared for the fair, my family endured many practice rounds. We still laugh about my first State Fair demonstration. I showed people how to save money by mixing up homemade versions of Bisquick®, hot cocoa, and seasoned salt. After completing each mix, I'd explain the cost savings and then I'd place the mix on a *faux* shelf and proudly proclaim, "It's on the shelf!" I practiced a lot, so we filled our shelves with mixes. I did this in 6th or 7th grade and recall still using my homemade version of Bisquick® in my senior year! Whenever my family is together and somebody is looking for something, my brother or sister will yell, "It's on the shelf!"

INGREDIENTS:

9 c. flour
¼ c. sugar
2-⅓ c. powdered milk
1T. salt
⅓ c. baking powder
2 c. shortening

DIRECTIONS:

In a lg. pan, stir the dry milk, baking powder, sugar and salt into the flour; mix thoroughly.

Cut the shortening into the dry ingredients until the mix is the consistency of corn meal.

Place the mix in a covered glass or plastic container and keep in a cool, dry place.

In warm weather the mix should be refrigerated.

Use within a month. Can be kept in the freezer.

To measure, pile the mix lightly into a cup and level off with a spatula or the back of a knife.

Taco Seasoning Mix

INGREDIENTS:

1 T. chili powder
2 t. onion powder
1 t. ground cumin
1 t. garlic powder
1 t. paprika
1 t. oregano
1 t. sugar
½ t. salt
1 t. cornstarch

DIRECTIONS:

Combine all ingredients.

Use as you would a 1-¼-oz. envelope of commercial taco seasoning.

To season 1 lb. of browned, drained ground beef, add ¾ c. water and simmer 5 minutes.

Kool Aid® Playdough

To celebrate my nieces' and nephews' birthdays, I invite them over for a little slumber party at my house. Usually, the party consists of a field trip, movie, craft project, and baking something yummy to take back to their siblings. (I usually need a day off after these slumber parties!) Here are a couple of creations we've made to play with during our slumber parties.

INGREDIENTS:

2 c. flour
2 pkg. unsweetened Kool-Aid® (adds color and scent)
1 c. salt
2 t. cream of tartar
⅓ c. oil
2 c. boiling water

DIRECTIONS:

Combine the ingredients in a mixing bowl.

Knead until the consistency of playdough is smooth.

Goo

INGREDIENTS:
8 oz. white glue
food coloring (optional)
1 c. water
1 T. 20 Mule Team® Borax

DIRECTIONS:
Combine glue, food coloring and ¾ c. water in a bowl.
In a separate bowl, combine 1 T. borax and ¼ c. water.
Add 2 T. of the Borax mixture to the glue mixture, stirring until a blob forms. Remove the blob.
Add another 2 T. of the Borax-and-water mixture to the glue mixture.
Repeat the process until the glue mixture is all gone. Knead the blobs together and store in an airtight container.

Josie's heart-shaped pizzas at her birthday slumber party with Auntie Boo

special thanks

I want to give special thanks to my Mom and Dad's family and friends. The prayers and supportive messages you all sent before, during and after Mom's mastectomy were so reassuring. When Dad and I waited with her before surgery, she was remarkably calm. Thanks to all the loving prayers you provided, she was able to relax and trust God. What a true gift! Thank you so much for all your support.

We didn't have much time to create this book, as we came up with the idea in January and knew we wanted to release it before Mother's Day. I benefited from many people who volunteered their time and talents to make this book a reality on a tight timeline, allowing me to balance it with my full-time job at Medtronic.

Rich Fischer, thanks so much for sharing your public relations expertise. Without you, nobody would know about our little project. Party Crashers Photography, thanks for accommodating a last-minute, early-morning photo session on a sub-zero Sunday morning. Thanks to our personal tailor, Jane Nordane who whipped up those great pink aprons for all of us…in RECORD time! Thanks also to a couple of talented and gifted writers, Lindsey Dickinson and Mike Roach; when I was stumped about how to say something, you always managed to take my words and make me sound good. While I wrote stories, Annie, Kayla, Amy Draxten and Emily Haugen tapped away at their keyboards to get all the recipes entered. Special thanks to Amy and Emily who planted the seed for this project and continue to keep me sane on a daily basis! And thank you to all of our friends who supported and encouraged us to do this… THANKS!

To Dara Moore and the crew at Beaver's Pond Press: This project was just an idea until I met you. Thanks so much for all your support throughout this project! Our editor, Jennifer Manion, is truly a magician; she somehow managed to bring some order and clarity to all these recipes! And to James Monroe, the designer who made the book look so good!

To Char and David at the Minnesota Affiliate of Susan G. Komen for the Cure®: Thanks for all your assistance and flexibility with this project, but more importantly, thanks for everything you do on a daily basis to help women fighting breast cancer and for all your efforts to help find a cure.

Finally, special thanks to our dear family friend, Uncle Pat: Thank you so much for your unbelievable generosity. Because of you more than $17 of every book sold will go directly to Susan G. Komen for the Cure®. You are *by far* our favorite Irish uncle!